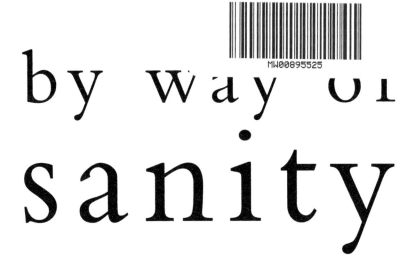

by way of
sanity

DR. LAUREN
WOODHOUSE

13 PRINCIPLES FOR

SUCCESSFUL LIVING

IN A CHAOTIC WORLD

Prentice Hall Canada
Scarborough, Ontario

Canadian Cataloguing in Publication Data

Woodhouse, Lauren J.
    By way of sanity

Includes bibliographical references and index.
ISBN 0-13-083048-8

1. Self-actualization (Psychology). I. Title.

BF637.S4W662 1999   158.1   C98-932446-X

© 1999 Lauren Woodhouse
Prentice-Hall Canada Inc., Scarborough, Ontario

Prentice-Hall, Inc., Upper Saddle River, New Jersey
Prentice-Hall International (UK) Limited, London
Prentice-Hall of Australia, Pty. Limited, Sydney
Prentice-Hall Hispanoamericana, S.A., Mexico City
Prentice-Hall of India Private Limited, New Delhi
Prentice-Hall of Japan, Inc., Tokyo
Simon & Schuster Southeast Asia Private Limited, Singapore
Editora Prentice-Hall do Brasil, Ltda., Rio de Janeiro

ISBN 0-13-083048-8

Director, Trade Group: Robert Harris
Acquisitions Editor: Dean Hannaford
Editor: Lenore d'Anjou
Assistant Editor: Joan Whitman
Production Coordinator: Shannon Potts
Art Direction: Mary Opper
Cover and Interior Design: Julia Hall
Cover Image: Photonica/W. Thompson
Page Layout: Joan Wilson

Epigraph from *True Stories*, copyright © Margaret Atwood 1981.
Reprinted by permission of Oxford University Press Canada.

1 2 3 4 5 W 02 01 00 99 98

Printed and bound in Canada

Visit the Prentice Hall Canada Web site! Send us your comments, browse our cata-
logues, and more. **www.phcanada.com**

About the Author

Lauren Woodhouse, PhD., D Psy., DD., possesses a rare blend of talents as a scientist and communicator. Not only is she is a gifted psychotherapist, but also an actress, athlete, pilot, and social critic. As a speaker, she has an uncanny ability to bring audiences to their knees with her dry humor and comic impersonations, while demonstrating the depth of her wisdom and empathy for the human spirit.

Born in Montreal, Dr. Woodhouse has lived and studied in a variety of locations in Canada, the United States, and Europe. She currently lives and practices in Ottawa, surrounded by friends, family, and her Golden Retriever.

The facts of this world seen clearly
are seen through tears;
why tell me then
there is something wrong with my eyes?
Margaret Atwood

Contents

Find, take time to, bear the frustration of ascertaining what obstacles are in the way of your loving yourself. This is a requisite for successful living.

To accelerate the process of self-acceptance, forgive both yourself and others— always, continuously, and with no exceptions related to the degree of the perceived attack or hurtful action.

Recognize your own fears, observe yourself with others, and admit that you are unnecessarily fearful—even if some people have given you reason to be. Health, healing, and the ability to love, even to be successful at whatever you are and do are only available to those who let go of fear.

Look for the depth of goodness and strengths (as well as the vulnerability) in others, rather than judging others for their fallibility.

Try to perceive the poor behavior of others as a call for help, an indication of fear or confusion, rather than as an attack or assault.

We are all teachers and students to each other. Some teachers and lessons are more harsh than others. Be aware of the lesson inherent in every interaction or relationship in the present as well as in successful or unsuccessful relationships from the past.

Preface

I have attempted to write a thoughtful and instructive book that reflects the linkages among the many aspects of our frequently hurried and harried lives. Throughout, I have also tried to address our inclination to hunker down in the face of contemporary challenges—including those related to ever-changing workplaces, family dilemmas, issues of partnership, and the western cultural anathema of diminishing youth.

A theme running through each chapter is the necessity of our finding the courage to both change and grow—regardless of our age, form of work, or hierarchical position. Whether at work amid the swirl of chaotic, continuous change, or at home, with challenges related to time and financial constraints, we can no longer take a facile approach to communication, interconnectedness, and community. We need to do the inner and outer work necessary to access and connect with our key resources—ourselves, and those with whom we work and live.

Now an urgent practical necessity, self-knowledge and the respectful recognition of others has long been the concern of easily dismissed theologians and of authors or speakers to whom, one sometimes feels, the average workplace or life challenge is a mere theoretical concept. However, for the average person and reader, there is nothing either dismissable or theoretical about the unpredictable exigencies and responsibilities of contemporary life and work.

This book contains working principles for both sane and successful living. But, just as importantly, it prescribes ways to manage changes in our work lives—changes that statistics show are proving to be intolerable, even crippling to a large portion of a seasoned working population. Ironically, many of us are emotionally handicapped at a time when workloads and demands for adaptability and creativity are greater than ever.

No one has fathomed or prepared us, in formal educational or training exercises, for the fact that we would have to, in essence, become all that we can be as talented, caring, and infinitely creative human animals. So it is understandable that most of us thought we could be and apply "half-selves" to our work and relationships, and take only partial responsibility for the fundamental facts of our lives.

In explaining and prescribing the 13 principles I write as a behaviourist, a practical theologian, and a consultant to a variety of associations, institutions, and corporations. The principles address key areas related and sometimes visceral to human performance. They also, overlappingly, direct attention to our shared suppression of fear; our understandable, interactive ineptitude; and our resistance to new, non-hierarchical models of life and work.

Untended to, we cannot succeed in a not-very-brave new world. And the tending has to come from ourselves. Then we can sensitively attend to each other, whether it be in the realm of personal relationships, or in valid, creative connections with those with whom we work.

Acknowledgments

In my two previous books, *Laughing in the Face of Change* and *Essential Adjustments*, I mentioned many individuals who had inspired and supported me through the arduous process of research and writing. Here I am thanking fewer people by name, but many more of you have a solid place in my heart. I can only hope that you know who you are.

I want to thank the participants in the hundreds of audiences I speak to each year; they learn and laugh with me, making my work and busy schedule a blessing. I should also acknowledge the sense of wonder and profoundly challenging dilemma brought to my life and work by Helen, Dyan, Paul, and the late Michael Carenza Conte. I pray for some time together. Thanks also to Carolann and Ted Regan of Regan Productions for having faith in me; Lynda Davies for reinforcing the fact that memorable souls live in our hearts; Mike Duffy for being a kind and generous addition to my life; Suzanne Hollick for facilitating an important professional connection; the late Walter Light, once chief executive officer of Northern Telecom and a coal miner's son, for always welcoming me into his family with warmth and fun; Dr. Enid Richey for helping to keep me going and touching my soul during an intense postgraduate experience; Jan Potter for being my buddy; John and Betty Harrison for long being an exemplar of responsible partnership; the late Shirley Snell for being tender with me when I was a child; Nancy Bean for leaving much laughter and continued work with troubled youth as her legacy; Carole Brickenden for her sense of honor and practiced Christianity; and the bright folk at the several and best professional speaking agencies in Canada and the United States with whom I have worked in the past year. I hope that we can continue to break new ground and to bring a new level of professionalism to a worthy business sometimes besmirched by lesser players than yourselves.

I have also benefited from heated discussions with individuals, powerful and powerless, whose articulation of and efforts toward the human requirements of the new order have added to both my ruminations and my inspiration. Among them are the souls and soldiers of organizational and personal change of the Royal Bank of Canada, Bell Canada, CUIS and CUMIS, the Alberta Treasury, Zengler Miller, the International Association of Business Communicators and its membership, West Coast Energy, Canada Trust, The Northern Group, Cantel-ATT, Energizer, the Ontario Recreational Educators Association, RJR Nabisco, and the dedicated people at the Canadian International Development Association.

Finally, I offer immeasurable gratitude to Lenore d'Anjou for her renowned skill as an editor and her wise, firm, and gentle way with authors; much appreciation to Karen Alliston for both adding to the quality of this manuscript and seeing it and me to its fruition; and thanks to Dean Hannaford for bringing me into the fold of Prentice Hall.

Introduction to the Principles

All human change requires that we have as clear a sense of where we are, as we do of where we want to be, and the effort required to get there.

Meister Eckhart

Most of the time, most of us feel as if we are faking sanity. A new millennium is upon us, a transitional time of momentous structural and social upheaval. Thirty years ago, B.F. Skinner predicted a pervading "cultural insanity," as had Erich Fromm, writing even earlier and using different terminology.

Today, their forecasts are proving true. Sensitive commentators frequently mention the speed of change and its effects on our rollercoaster world. Peter Drucker, writing in the November 1994 issue of *The Atlantic Monthly,* referred to the "revolutionary transformation" of our brief lives in an incredibly, impossibly short period of time. Except in times of war, no society has ever before had to adjust to, cope with, and manage such radical alterations in individuals' inner and outer worlds. Dramatic and constant lifestyle changes are now and forever demanded of us and our institutions. Moreover, we have never had so many and so few tools with which to manage internal and external adaptations.

In large part because of our defensive reactions in the face of interminable change and apparent social insecurity, something is happening among us and to us that isn't pretty or healthy. Politely adversarial, we are *pretending* to be okay, but we are watching our backs as if we were on a most-wanted list. We fear just about everything, especially what seems to be the omnipresence of danger and bad guys or adversaries. Where are the good guys? And if *we* are the good guys (and gals), what the heck are we doing? Why are we hiding from each other, and either hurting or ignoring others with such reflexive consistency? After all, no one has an edge over anyone else. We are living and working in social and organizational conditions that none of us has ever faced before. Studies show that we have backed off and away from each other, remaining just close enough to view each other peripherally with suspicion. As a result of this defensive posturing, much that is critical to our ability to cope and succeed is missing from our protectively structured and strictured lives.

Many people today are making a great deal of money recommending a multitude of simple approaches to "new-age" living. But most, perhaps understandably, are avoiding the real issues at the heart of human behavior, historic and modern, especially as it manifests itself in crisis. What sells in the way of how-to publications is what most of us seem to be searching for: something to soothe us, to make us happy, and to ensure the efficient suppression of our emptiness. Few if any voices speak directly to the dire need for responsible management of our humanity.

Until recently, a quick read, a good shopping spree, or a new car could go a long way (for a short time) toward enabling us to "do life" more bearably. Now, however, the honest and seriously concerned among us realize that *things* don't do it for us anymore, and we are looking elsewhere for simple fixes.

Not coincidentally, we have available a plethora of literature that promises simple techniques to acquiring bucks and inner beauty and offers scintillating sink-to-success stories featuring celebrity exemplars who have ridden the crests and endured the valleys of modern living. In fact, we have made self the latest commodity to buy and ingest as an elixir against authentic self-development. We fall for the easy pursuit of happiness rather than face the work involved with managing our misery or dissatisfaction. Just as Prozac has come to play a social role in millennial living, so has the cosmetic dressing up of self. Indeed, we have even commodified spirituality, as if it too were something that we can take for quick self-mollification. We are dangerously attracted to speedy but ersatz, microwave versions of processed growth and maturity, which, in reality, must be hard won.

Moreover, the locus of attention in the avalanche of today's curative advice, whether it is aimed at the individual or our roles in organizations, is on *self* and *self alone,* not on the complexity and triumph of connections. In fact, we are so focused on ourselves that we are losing our Selves, as well as those who would be with us in love and work. We want surface fixes, practical and safe albeit pithy or poetic, that guarantee that we won't really have to feel who we are and what we have become: frantic, frightened doers in a seemingly valueless and ruthless global arena. We also want insurance against having to face our need for and increasing lack of meaningful relationships.

In brief, we are losing our selves and our sanity. A large majority of the working population is insecure, frightened, and toiling in rote obedience to old rules and work styles. We have difficulty remembering data, we struggle to use technology that didn't exist two months ago, and we strain to remember our children's birthdays. Moreover, everyone seems to be questioning our ability to cope. As a result, both the sincere and the slick are getting involved with providing either earnest advice or trite salvos for our ills.

Yet virtually nothing that is currently available for a wide audience addresses the depth of the many critical issues related to modern, transitional living. Without discomfiting, in-depth discussions and nonmedical, nonacademic literature on the subject of "us in a new era," we have nowhere to go. And without a healthy allegiance to shared principles, basic behavioral imperatives, boundaries, and a common, fundamentally new modus operandi for life and work in a not necessarily brave new world, our behavior has become more extreme, even when it is dressed up in the polite tension of political correctness.

The fact that many have lost track of what is important to life and living is bad enough. But now, during these years of millennial upheaval, the problem shows. Not only is it evident that we are lost, anxious, and fearfully isolated from each other, but we are *behaving* as if we are frightened and lost. Like frightened animals, we are becoming vigilant, defensive, and poised for conflict. The circumstances seem to have upped the ante. We have—or *think* we have—more reason than ever to be poised in rigid self-defense. This tightening disintegration of the human spirit calls for more than a reader-friendly "steps for success" book. It requires a revolution in thought and behavior, the how-to of which is beyond what we have ever before had to think about, let alone consciously aspire to and act on.

Long in the Coming

In this forever period of unpredictability and revolutionary change, many of us who are at what should be the peak of our earning power are more like toddlers taking a first swim in white water rapids. Moreover, caught up in a world that is still highly competitive (in spite of what many organizations and corporations are espousing in the way of consensus and cooperation), many of us are faking competency and barely repressing percolating anger.

In fact, we are more in competition with each other than ever—and significantly more ruthless. The number of "traditional jobs"—those we were trained and educated to expect to have for a lifetime—is shrinking faster every year (at a rate unforseen by the best of the futurists to whom we listened with unctuous comfort in the early 1980s). Now much of what we are doing is changing daily, and we are expected to learn new tricks every hour on the hour or become unemployable—the depersonalized linguistic equivalent of fat-free unemployment. At the same time, we have to learn to work better, in "flow"—that is, in a state of ease—with ourselves, and more synergistically with other (fewer) people more of the time. All this, when most of us, until the very recent past, could function without too much concern for our behavior, our ethics, or even the fundamental effect we had on those around us, as long as *we* felt secure. For years, we could get away with merely doing our jobs, pushing and prodding for success and consuming as much as we could, including, symbolically speaking, other people.

Making a Heartful Journey

The principles I offer in this book are not, needless to say, a panacea for all that this latest human, social, and technological revolution has brought us. They are merely guidelines and ultimately instructions that if followed daily with commitment and consistent application, can transform our daily personal and work lives, as well as the processes, practices, and interactions therein. But they will not work unless we *choose* to use them and to become involved in the intensely personal issues and processes related to them.

A long time ago, we lost track of why we are doing what we are doing and for whom. We have grown ever more systemically alienated from each other, coming to see each other as potential enemies, rather than as brothers and sisters sharing identical fears, dreams, and needs for love and belongingness. When one considers what scientists have proven about how miraculously similar human beings are in makeup, it seems incredible that we can have become so mutually separating and pragmatically uncaring, that while struggling with transformation and insecurity, we so reflexively yet strategically turn on each other in order to stay in the ever-changing game. Doing so hurts us. We must relearn that we are turning on the only aspect of life—others and love—that can truly support and help us.

The principles described here are designed to address the fact that we have reached a point at which we dare not bring our hearts to life. That is, at a time in history when heartful living, heartful interaction, and creativity are more important than ever (when were they not important?), we are more estranged and closed than ever. We hunker down in fear and confusion, questioning our ability to sustain what feels increasingly like fraudulent competency and postured confidence.

Studies show that even before we were asked to change, improve, learn, and grow—by tomorrow—most of us were unsure of our usefulness or value. Now, many feel as if the game is up, as if our imposture will be revealed and punished. We are stuck in old perceptual constructs and beliefs, cultural, personal, intellectual, and emotional. As a result, we are paralyzed when faced with real change. Our ability to act toward meeting the needs of the new order as well as ourselves (and each other) in that order are thus limited. We have to free ourselves of antiquated notions regarding work and life and of notions about ourselves in relation to others.

Erich Fromm predicted it. So did a variety of other psychologists and social scientists, including Abraham Maslow, Hans Selye, Eric Erickson, Karl Marx, and even John Kenneth Galbraith. In various ways, they warned that we would become so involved in the means of production that we would lose ourselves. Moreover, we would come to worship the material things that we acquire by merely working to rule at an income-producing activity. This seduction would work for us, as well as for society and its commercial and public institutions, *for a while.*

Little was demanded of us in the past. Little of our brains, of our individual geniuses, let alone of our hearts had to be brought to the then-separate dimension of our lives that we call work. For the most part, all we had to do was *show up and show*—"do doing" in a way that fit with the particular ethos in which we chose to place ourselves. Only the exceptional people, those who were once snickeringly referred to as *weird,* quietly persisted with new, creative, and heartful endeavors of a truly personal kind. Most of us, trained in obedience, in the security that comes with inaction, and in a cultivated absence of emotional expression and involvement, are now trapped in lessons well learned. And the eccentrics, the Bill Gateses of the world, should be our models, not because of their wealth but because of their passion, their ability to risk doing, being wrong, and doing again, and because they truly communicate and connect in order to access creativity and genius in themselves and others.

Working, Living, and Working

Thus, we have not dared to bring much of our hearts to our lives. And we have remained or become inauthentic in our work lives. Now, however, more is demanded of us than the once-common, mechanical way in which we were able to go about acquiring a paycheck.

Indeed, more is now demanded of us than is immediately evident to our traditional mindset. Hans Selye, often called the father of stress, emphasized that unless our work is part of our lives and our living is done at work, we can produce nothing of value.

Moreover, he pointed out, we will sicken and die young. The creation of separate selves for work and life is the "killer stress," he said, a contorted version of human life. Presenting separate, monitored, false selves for work and life cannot meet either the human needs for meaningful labor and creativity or the equally vital needs for human love, play, and companionship.

The implications of what has been known for decades (even centuries) about the necessity of integrating our lives should hearten us. The changes we have to make bear no relation to inauthentic quarterly corporate cant. They are changes that will, by necessity, warm and open our hearts—and save our lives.

Getting Real

The changes that we are being asked to make as organizational and social participants are merely beneath the surface of buzz phrases and ever-changing organizational chants. The "cup-a-soup" (expensive but empty) trend-of-the-month approach popular in the 1980s has, fortunately, long been discarded. Our society and its institutions have hit a critical point amid a global rush that has left us at a point of no return—as a planet, as nations, and as individuals.

This critical point is actually a fundamental wakeup call. Those of us in the western world who have been living with the expectation of regular remuneration, secure if excessive consumption, and automatic companionship are in a state of insult and trauma. The crisis has been long in the coming. And as challenging as it is, it is an opportunity the likes of which we have not had in generations. Now, we *have* to reset our priorities, direct and manage our "beingness," and address ourselves to creative, value-full endeavors of the human spirit. And we can't necessarily do that in four easy steps.

The principles in this book address the fundamental obstacles both to successful living generally and to succeeding in the new millenium. As computer engineers scramble to find ways to save data and to support informational systems vital to commercial processes, social scientists, humanists, and theologians ponder new ways of human *being*. Much of what we seek, we already know but have forgotten, or have been permitted to leave unused in the always complex process of living.

As participants in processes of surviving the crunch of change, we will never again be permitted to be the same, to be less than we are. As our institutions and our leaders struggle to restructure faltering enterprises, we now have to redevelop the flexibility, fearlessness, and creativity that are natural dimensions of our humanity. That is all we are being asked to do. We need to unlearn the lessons of passivity, competition, and passionless daily living by rote, regulation, and logic. We must reexperience the stimulation of ordered chaos and creative decision making. We also have to relearn closeness, cooperation, and trust. We have lived and worked too long in adversary and competition, to the documented detriment of our humanity.

We have to do—or at least start—all this *now*. We have an opportunity to rehumanize the many, currently inhumane dimensions of what are empty but harried existences.

We also have a chance to avoid becoming sad statistics of modern life. To resist finding the new way is to die resisting—spiritually, literally, or both. This, scientists are proving. To search for a return to what we are and do at our best is to reflourish and re-create as individuals and communities. This, life has taught for thousands of years.

Becoming Us

We have become the bad guys or, at the very least, the human and emotional obstacles in the way of positive change. We ourselves create fear and rigidity in the face of new and unforseen challenges. And as a consequence of our panicky desire to hold on to what had worked for us, to what we had accumulated, and to what had seemed controllable, we have taken our terror out on each other. Just when human hearts are starved for affirmation, trust, and comfort, we are dishing out pain as if we were in a desperate, primitive scramble for survival. We have to center ourselves, take stock, and relearn how to work and live with each other in entirely new (and some old) ways. Moreover, we have to start by working on ourselves—not merely brushing up on, but re-creating ourselves from the inside out.

For many years, I have been studying eastern and western philosophy and spirituality. These journeys, along with my continued studies in various dimensions of human behavior, have lead to the distillation of years of notes, papers, discussions, and meditations into the 13 principles offered here. They encompass an enormous mass of overlapping wisdom, philosophy, science, and historic human truths. They are not the stuff of rocket science. But that is the point. They are life principles, parameters of sanity and survival that, in many branches of human science, represent undisputed facts—the essence of the very little that we can call *truth*. And as truths, they are guidelines for earnest human endeavors of a visceral, committed, and effortful kind.

Some Practical Points

Much of what I am asking readers to do is simple but requires both effort and courage. Consequently, I offer a few notes about the book and how to use it.

A Caveat about 13

An awkward, even inordinate number of the principles in this book are related to an awkward and inordinate process of unbecoming and resetting who, how, and what we are going to be from here on in.

When I sorted out my notes and thoughts, they fell into 13 principles. For generations, many people in our culture have superstitiously perceived that number as unlucky, seriously or half-seriously avoiding it, fearful of what they think of as its activity negativity. Yet other people regard it—equally superstitiously—as a lucky number.

So when I discovered I had 13 principles in need of discussion, I decided I would neither arbitrarily limit them to 12 nor manufacture another to bring the number to 14. Either course would have both perpetuated a prevailing view (propelling or impeding belief) and censored this writing in a way directly contradicting my overall objective. Moreover, I would have affected and probably restricted my work because of my fear of people's fears of a mere number. I do not want to live that way, nor do I want to create and teach accordingly.

From a more lighthearted, yet realistic perspective, all we have to do is to decide that in a millennium in which none of us has before lived, the number 13 is positive, lucky, or, *sanely* just another number.

Two More Caveats

Readers should be aware that the use of the pronouns *he* and *she* throughout this book is deliberately varied and arbitrary. Unless specified, it in no way implies that one gender is inclined to a specific behavior more than the other.

Also be aware that the case studies I use represent real situations and real people. The names and some inconsequential circumstances have been changed to protect the identity of the individuals and organizations involved.

A Note of Explanation

Finally, some readers may find useful a clarification of the varying use of *self* and *Self* in these pages. When modern behaviorists employ the word *self*, we are referring to that part of us humans that functions with mundane, habitual consciousness in our everyday lives. It represents the regulated, trained, and ego-centered manifestation of who we are as a result of socialization and personal experience.

In contrast, *self* or *oneself* refers to that transcendent part of us: the thinking, insightful reflexively compassionate part of us that goes outside of or beyond everyday patterns created by cognitive, emotional, and behavioral programming. Once uncomfortable with the usage, I now use the term in good scientific company. As a result of ongoing studies of the peculiarity of the superathlete, debriefings of long-held hostages, increasing medical research into near-death experiences, and the documented experiences of survivors of technically unsurvivable disasters, the medical, scientific, and social science communities are in firm agreement as to the existence, commonality, and infinite value of the human *Self*.

How to Use This Book

I suggest that this book be read in sections, pondered, acted on, and then read through in sequence again, so that what readers learn about themselves, including the necessity of change from the inside out, takes hold and becomes a part of the rubric of their perceptions and behaviors.

Each principle is articulated at the beginning of its chapter, where it is represented by a title and by a few lines about its pertinence to specific dimensions of individuals' overlapping work and personal lives.

At the end of each chapter are a case study and an exercise. The short vignettes are real examples about real people, bringing to life the customized use of each of the principles.

The exercises will be most beneficial if they are done or practiced for a week at a time during a second reading of the book. This method will help readers focus on the specific principle and make it a living reality; it will also cause inner change as a result of its practical application to daily circumstances and interactions. The order in which the principles are positioned for discussion and practiced application is far from random. Rather, they lead logically one to the next, and readers conceptually interconnect them, consciously or unconsciously. Moreover, the last principle may be the most useful in that it focuses on a method of redirecting the human psyche, one that depends on having accepted the previous points.

I also suggest that the principles be read in peace, "far from the madding crowd," with time taken to just read, to be, and to feel what is personally pertinent and potentially transformational.

A Final Note

Finally, may that which is of an energetic, higher power enable the reader to be open, to be touched and motivated by that which has been written here. It has been written with earnest love and concern for the millions of us who are struggling to merely stay sane, unaware of the comfort in the proven scientific powers and possibilities inherent in the practiced recognition of an "us."

With openness and courage, let us proceed.

Principle 1
Self-Acceptance

Find, take time to, bear the frustration of ascertaining what obstacles are in the way of your loving yourself. This is a requisite for successful living.

The most vulnerable and at the same time the most unconquerable thug is human self-love. Indeed, it is through being challenged that its power grows, and can, in the end, be the driving force of a life truly lived.

Nietzsche

Let us start with a common example. Last year, I met a beautiful, intelligent woman and her husband. The woman had a magically warm and childlike air about her, as if she had missed the lesson on withholding and aloofness. Her successful husband, an enlightened corporate executive, loves his work and respects those who work for him but finds his major joy in his family, and, in particular, his wife and life partner.

This couple is, I assume, contented. But one small yet significant vulnerability mars their otherwise wonderful life together. The exceptional woman, mother, and partner cannot believe in or trust her good fortune. That is, she cannot believe that her "goodness" will last, that something won't happen to her husband or to one of her two healthy and successful children or that some other calamity won't come along. As a result, she misses a large portion of her deserved joy by worrying about whether, how, and when "it" will happen—when her good life will come tumbling down.

Emotionally, if not rationally, this fine woman would disagree with the adage, "You can never be too happy." From an emotional perspective, she would submit that one should hold back happiness, sandbag oneself *in case* there is a life- or joy-destroying flood. She can't believe in her "goodness" or accept that it will last. Either she does not believe that she deserves her blessings, or she does not trust in life itself.

Grace and Giving

Some lives are just graced. Like this couple, those beneath the umbrella of joy are invariably sweet, responsible, caring, and contributing souls. What some of them do not realize is that they, by virtue of their grace, *give as much if not more* than that with which they have been graced. If anyone ever thinks that he has been too lucky, or things have been too easy, he should take some time to think about how people feel with him, how many people have come to him for comfort over the years, and how many dear friends he has made and kept. Doesn't he inspire otherwise busy people, like myself, to pause to love him, to stay in touch, to want to be with him?

It rarely occurs to those with self-questioned grace that they give to the hidden lonely or to the recently injured among us, that they inadvertently and advertently give more to others precisely *because* they were and are graced with a life lacking in major tragedy or inordinate loss. In short, their unspoken but powerful emission of love is considerably more accessible and generously shared as a result of the calmer, more beautiful waters on which they do their living.

Fear and Self-Love

I opened with this example because it typifies how fearful we are of accepting, with a sense of deservedness, those good things that come into our lives. Our feelings of undeservedness stem from an emphasis on self-denial and self-denunciation that is primarily culturally induced. Further, so much has been written about self-love, especially since the 1980s, that many of us are sick of Teflon-coated messages about perfecting our lives in five easy steps.

In truth, few of us *choose* to hate ourselves and to be at daily war with ourselves. Most of us would choose a full, exciting, and loving life if we thought we could. But the myriad simplistic, albeit rhythmically Gibranian solutions are oft-times insulting, not to mention disappointing, when applied to the frustration and pain of self-denial. The easy, poetic answers are also more than somewhat spurious, given the extremely complex and epidemic nature of the problem. Most people who have read even the most promising works end up liking themselves even less for not liking themselves more after the reading experience. A losing game—and a not very playful one at that.

The Most Critical Trap

That said, it is, however, a truism that we cannot function as fully expressive human beings while we hate or are indifferent to the inner workings of our psyches and hearts—our beingness in the world. Self-care and self-love are the essential elements that enable us to connect with others by accepting ourselves. Self-love creates a mirror image of others that is loving. Self-hate mirrors itself as well.

Depending on the situation and the degree of intimacy, these intrapsychic mirrors mean that we can be open to and feel the essence of another human being who stands in our loving reflection. Conversely, we can shut down in unconscious fear of the reflection of that which we hate. We set this repetitive trap by ourselves for ourselves, but it also catches anyone who comes into emotional proximity.

Fear

Even if we know we are fearful and hard on ourselves, it is important to understand where some of these feelings came from. Early in our development, we were taught to self-punish and to play down our strengths and goodness. Inadvertently, the salient adults in our lives assigned us self-concepts when we were too powerless to understand or to resist generational programming. In an earnest attempt to both raise and tame us, we were all told no more than yes, that we were wrong more than we were right. As a result, even in the best of imperfect families, little beings were—and still are—programmed for an adulthood in which masking insecurities and negative self-concepts is the norm. Encouraged and, in some cases, pushed to succeed, especially monetarily, we "strut and fret" into a role that, on the one hand, enforces the repression and camouflage of our true Selves (our true, interconnected, and higher selves) and, on the other hand, was designed to ensure personal success in another era.

In other words, the socialization processes of the western world, especially North America, prepared us, as children, to participate in the old social and economic structures, but they left us false Selves, dragging the ball and chain of a lack of self-acceptance and self-love, which has always made it very difficult to succeed with ease and integrity. Now, in the shadow of a new millennium, just living—let alone making a living—has become so complex that we must live cleanly and clearly so as to maintain our sanity. We can no longer strain to camouflage our self-defined fraudulence or lack of okayness in the world.

Some individuals broke early (when sick leave and fiscal latitude for burnout breaks were still available). Even when things were considerably simpler, they had devotedly worked to rule, exerting themselves to prove themselves worthy while detesting every move they made—and themselves while they made them. Those of us who have maintained true grit longer are just luckier or have more physical stamina, or, indeed, are so petrifyingly programmed with self-doubt and insecurity that we have been able to endure a few more years of handicapped and handicapping pseudo-productivity.

Self-Hatred and Sabotage

Although I understand why talking about self-love is so difficult in our culture, I still find it hard to understand how many people continue to function without this fundamental dimension of healthy human living. In the medium or long term, self-hating people are not successful, either monetarily or in their work-related or personal relationships. When they meet and interact with others, they mirror their hatred, making it

4

impossible for those others to be able to be who *they* are, rather than the people the self-haters imagine in accord with their own inner fears and self-contempt.

In other words, because we project our lack of self-acceptance onto the world, we *cannot* connect, cooperate, or even deal honestly and openly with other human beings including our colleagues and our families. Further, if we hate ourselves, we have a built-in expectation that others will do the same. Therefore, we function in the world as hated beings, keeping our heads low to avoid what we perceive as inevitable, punitive blows to an undeserving Self.

Those among us who function without self-love are also prone to the more overt forms of self-sabotage. As self-haters, we do not believe we deserve or are allowed to succeed, to have financial security, or to enjoy the support of loved ones. So we virtually guarantee ourselves outcomes that confirm our secret sense of unworthiness. We also continue to involve ourselves in patterns of behavior and in situations that guarantee confirmation of our mordant belief.

Love, Which Attracts Love

In contrast, those of us with self-love—the result of a remarkably positive childhood or of hard work and attentiveness to the inner Self later in life—attract from others goodness, love, and the best they can offer. People with a healthy, fundamental foundation of self-love represent that envied minority of individuals who seem to get along with everyone and to have all things come to them with ease. They are generally happy, and they rarely fear anything less than a volcanic eruption or a nuclear accident.

These people are, however, so unusual that the majority in a suspicious and conventionally self-hating culture look at them with both awe and envy, and the latter too often turns into attack. We have all experienced, personally or by observation, the assaults to which seemingly comfortable people are subjected. Given our early lessons, we tend to mistrust those who have become happily productive and contributing participants in their professions and communities. These magnificent souls *need* to be in service to others, partially because they are able to recognize their blessings. In contrast, a self-hating or even self-ignoring individual has nei-

5

ther the inclination nor the energy to go beyond the limits of subsistence. A person who lacks self-acceptance accepts nothing about others that could stand as a tempting or action-inducing exemplar of a joyful commitment to heartful, intense, personal contribution.

In short, the self-haters believe that neither they nor most others have anything to give. They exist day to day in passive-aggressive criticism of themselves and others, plotting and sabotaging in reaction to their angry, sad, and self-limited lives.

Worthiness

Whether or not we can come to accept ourselves depends on whether or not we can come to feel worthy of our own love, let alone that of others. So many years and so much effort have inadvertently been put into making us feel unworthy, self-doubting, and insecure. But now we are adults, and *the job of living is ours alone*—with, if we are lucky, more than a little help from an energy or otherness that many of us believe promotes love, abundance, and security.

The key is not more material wealth, adversarial triumph, or other questionable if common victories. Rather, the key is personal, mental and emotional activity between self and Self. We can recondition ourselves to cultivate new self-concepts that both undo and redo our self-image, correcting our general sense of emptiness and unworthiness in the world. No one is stopping us from tending to our inner worlds; no one any longer has the power or influence to tell us who we are, *unless* we let someone do so.

Listening as If You Care

Listen to how you treat your Self, that inner part of you that is hidden but reflects upon the world. Listen as if you were listening to a small child suffering and fearful over his lack of worth, value, goodness, and ultimate security. Think of what you would say to the child and how you would be around him as a model and a support. Then, look in a mirror, at the child, and say something mollifying and assuring. Go as far as to mourn for the child in you who has suffered in hidden loneliness, and tend to him.

You are the most impressive voice and the most powerful influence in your life. You are also your greatest, perhaps only, nurturer and advocate. Retake and revive your Self and your life by doing the truly sacred inner work of self-salvation. Focus on it, but do not turn it into work. Do not push and set parameters of success and failure. Just be with the child, tend to his (your) wounds, and create and maintain a tender relationship free of self-flagellation and paralysis.

We must form a healthy relationship with our Selves to remain creatively self-connected in order to do the heady things that are asked of us as participants in an arguably insane new world. We need us.

Transcendence of Mere Selfhood

Most of us have either been turned off by institutionalized religion or pestered by the ostensibly spiritual. Consequently, we have to find our own path toward comprehending that aspect of humanity that exists beyond and detached from the material world.

Many would be surprised to know that the vast majority of the most successful people in the world have a strong sense of spiritual purpose. In fact, many wise and successful souls agree that spirituality *is* sanity. The dictates of the material world are too overwhelming for us without the use of our distinctly human propensity for transcendence. As magnificent and complex mammalian cerebrators, we are, more often than not, ego-driven rather than heart-driven. We need to be driven primarily from the heart and the soul in order to function in a consistent state of grace.

The Sense of Perfection

As we age, many of us become more connected with the transcendent details around us, including the perfection of nature and our oneness with others. And in our senior years, we are more likely to ask for help, to try to believe, and to be open to support from something other than our institutions, our associates, and our own increased individual efforts. Not surprisingly, later in life we also receive clear(er) answers to our calls and a grounding sense of our perfection in our place in creation.

Is it any mystery why those of us who seek support and sustenance from something other than the vagaries of position power, the stock market, and possessions fare far better than those who do not? People who view themselves as created for a purpose, who believe that there is some reason for their periods of light and darkness, joy and sadness, gain and loss have a head start on self-acceptance.

Today, more people, even younger people, are seeking out their purpose as well as their wider connection to and with life. Life, many are learning, is both a source of support and a source of self-definition and direction. The April 1997 issue of *Newsweek Magazine* presented, as its cover story, "The Power of Prayer." The article described the scientifically measurable effects of prayer and spirituality in general, but it also pointed to the increasing number of scientists, physicians, managers, and other professionals who are bringing spirituality into their previously atheistic existences, as well as into their life's work. Perhaps we all need scientific proof in order to muster even a little bit of faith. It is, however, only a "little bit" that we need to accelerate our processes of becoming—that is, to open up new dimensions in the complex avenues of the human psyche and to clarify who and what we are in the essential scheme of things.

In the same lighted places, we find help for our humanity, inner guidance as to how to make life easier and more fulfilling. That this is provided to us makes sense. Life could not possibly be meant to be as hard, painful, and seemingly futile as it is commonly experienced. The life pattern of work-sleep-work-sleep-holiday and start all over again that we have designed and committed ourselves to sustaining is not even a half-life. It is a dehumanizing routine that frames and directs what are often deliberately dormant spirits. We are too capable, too grand to be self-imprisoned by mere human invention—even if the invention is our lives and the invention our own.

The Fruit of Self-Acceptance

In addition to the emotional-mental activity that we must conduct in order to free ourselves of false and self-diminishing self-concepts, we must, at some point, consider asking for help. My greatest strengths in times of unbearable pain have come from a combination of inner cognitive work and an openness to inspiration, explanation, and clarification from something apart from the materiality of the problem.

I cannot detach myself when I am in a state of pain, grief, anger, or frustration. None of us can. Yet something else about our beingness can do so. There is order and loving sanity in this part of our Selves to which we can go by virtue of who and what we are. Regardless of what one calls it—the Holy Spirit or Jung's collective unconscious—it exists for and of us all. We merely have to be still and listen for it—and then accept the comfort and order it brings to our inner chaos and troubled hearts.

This is a fact. Scientific research has proven us capable of drawing from a source or an energy that is instantly clarifying of who and what we are and how valuable we are to creation. We merely have to listen with nothing more or less than healthy skepticism.

Indeed, even with our lives increasingly strained by the vagaries of social and organizational adjustment, working toward self-acceptance can help us to grow in relationships and units critical to new and mandatorily changing roles. Work can and should be an intimate, personally expressive, and humanly demanding endeavor. Further, success does not come to those who mismanage themselves because of self-disdain. If we have not accepted ourselves—that is, deemed ourselves worthy of success, friendship, a followership, or at least a modicum of acclaim—we cannot succeed or contribute in any legitimate, lasting way. We can merely build on our own self-contempt and inadvertently add to that of others.

It is incumbent upon us, *for us,* to do the mental work necessary for self-acceptance and self-love. And much of that work can be done in mere moments of solitude and silence. We can test and retest the clarifying power of stillness and self-attentiveness by daring to exclude deflecting distractions. If, in silence, we eventually feel loved and safe, we are tapping into that which created us perfectly—already accepted, guiltless, and deserving of joy.

By practicing in silence as well as in pensive moments throughout the day, we get used to a new feeling or sense of basic okayness. We must then frame the feeling and induce it often, concurrent with mental and material amendments. And in the not-too-distant future, without even knowing it, we can find ourselves basking in the light of a new beginning founded on what really is the greatest and most important love of all—that which exists quietly and powerfully between a self and a Self.

CASE STUDY

Joyce Takes a Rough Road to Self-Acceptance

Joyce came from a home in which both parents loved her but were very strict and distinctly unaffectionate. They provided her with all the advantages a young lady could want. She went to a fine private school, attended dance, piano, and etiquette classes, and was forced to join a tennis and a debating club. Her parents wanted the best for her and for her to be the best.

Joyce was, however, extremely shy and very uncoordinated. She loved animals and secretly took care of three kittens in her backyard. She dutifully performed her mother's wishes at classes and clubs, but she counted the seconds until she could return home to play with her cats, read, or do her homework. Her entire elementary and secondary school life was spent attempting to gain her mother's and father's approval, as well as her demanding teachers'. But she never felt that she met the standards she was supposed to meet.

When Joyce went away to the university of her parents' choice, she started to unravel. She had been so used to attempting to please that she made pathetic, if well-meaning gestures to other students to serve them in some way so as to gain their acceptance and friendship. She could not function without approval, and she did not know how to live without attempting to acquire it. Joyce not only had difficulty with self-acceptance; she did not even know what it was. Everything she had done, she had done for others, and she continued to apply this modus operandi at school. Needless to say, she put many people off and felt increasingly unacceptable and as if she were an outsider—just as she had, she admitted in therapy, her whole life.

After a while, Joyce secretly sought therapy because of suicidal thoughts. She had come to hate herself for never measuring up and was tired of the race to be approved. She was even fearful that her parents would hate her if she took her life. They would know for sure that she was an abject failure.

Joyce had had no opportunity to explore who she really was, unencumbered by the ambitions and definitions of others. She felt empty and apart from others because she had had no opportunity to form an identity. Although she went into therapy because of her wish to take her own life, she soon realized that the problem was that she did not have one to take. She did not know who she was or what she enjoyed and had never had a chance to put herself forward as a person to be liked and enjoyed. Indeed, she had to learn that she was allowed to be here on earth as much as everyone else and that she need not please anyone but herself. In short-term therapy, she almost had to be rereared in order to feel okay as merely Joyce, without all the appurtenances of someone else's definition of success.

Years later, with her Self intact, Joyce became a successful lawyer. Her parents were thrilled, yet to Joyce, their pride mattered very little. She was finally proud *of herself* and liked who she was. She loved the law and stayed with it after she married and had children. Today she is a US district court judge.

Joyce is no longer invisible. But she had to reach a crisis point in her life, a time when she literally did not want to go on living, before she could see the major problem and work on it. Indeed, she found that not only did she lack self-acceptance but also that she had never really accepted others either. She was too busy trying to please them and, as a result, was both blind to their individuality and angry with them for making her have to try so hard to gain favor. Not surprisingly, she found that once she accepted who and what she was, others suddenly became much more likable, not to mention undemanding and emotionally generous.

EXERCISE

Look into your own eyes several times a day and note what you see. Undoubtedly, you will find determination, sadness, the potential for joy, even innocence. Experiment with going about your days with this image of you, a separate person, in mind. Note how much kinder you are tempted to be once you see yourself as a feeling, sensitive, longing Self.

Principle 2

Forgiveness and Acceptance

To accelerate the process of self-acceptance, forgive both yourself and others—always, continuously, and with no exceptions related to the degree of the perceived attack or hurtful action.

If we could read the secret history of our enemies we should find in each man's life sorrow and suffering enough to disarm all hostility.
Henry Wadsworth Longfellow

The two most important words in the English language are *fear* and *forgiveness,* and the former commonly acts as a deterrent to the latter. Consciously or unconsciously, too many of us live too often in the grip of fear. In fact, fearfulness, a barrier to all things courageous and humane, is so common that both the word and the act of forgiveness have all but left our verbal and behavioral vocabularies.

The profound, heart-pressing squeeze we experience as victims of the actions of others takes a greater toll on our lives than all other life stressors combined. Because we are brilliantly (and disastrously) creative, complex, cognitive creatures, forgiveness should have been among our first lessons. However, it was not. Instead, we are all well trained in suspicion and vengefulness. The media delight us with stories of comeuppance, and many of us can hold a grudge longer than it took our primitive ancestors to invent the wheel. We are avengers, not forgivers, and not very adept avengers at that.

At this point in human history, as well as in our individual histories, we feel that we have more to be angry about than ever, that we have somehow been cheated and tricked by life and social institutions. We have become particularly sensitive to the actions of others, even our friends, somehow suspecting and expecting that they too will turn on, disappoint, or fail us. In fact, I have had patients who felt relief upon finally being crossed by one of their last, remaining friends or by their latest spouse. The anticipation of being hurt was worse than the emotionally familiar reality of its actually happening. When the expectation was fulfilled, these patients felt they had fewer people to lose. Moreover, with no one left to keep an eye on, everyone remaining in their arid sphere fell into a safer, tidier mental-emotional category. Yet they were more unhappy than ever. Little did they know that what they had left to worry about unconsciously were the vagaries of an empty life and the enemy of an angry, victimized self.

Soul Erosion

The most soul-eroding experience that the human body, mind, and spirit can experience is inaction on the need for forgiveness. It hardens our hearts, literally and figuratively, and stifles all that is creative and naturally brilliant about us. To not forgive (or not know how to forgive) is tantamount to having a terminal illness. Isolated in repressed pain and attenuated anger, the conscious and unconscious pressure of having clumps of unforgiven people in our lives eats away at us, weakens us, and then kills us in a variety of ugly ways and stages. The greater the number of people we condemn, the more isolated we become from our humanity or from ourselves, and from *all* others.

Self-Forgiveness: A Start

To choose to forgive is to merely know ourselves sufficiently well to be able to identify with those who hurt us advertently or inadvertently—

that is, to see the misactions of others as our own potential misactions. This is a skill of intelligent personhood.

First and foremost, we have to forgive ourselves, whether we have committed an offense against someone or not. I hear again and again, both from my private patients and from individuals across the continent, that they feel profoundly guilty without any concrete reason for their feelings. And I routinely ask these good people why they feel so guilty. When their brows furrow, I make suggestions. Have they robbed a bank? Are they seasoned kidnappers? Do they regularly shoplift or steal from their companies? Have they ever deliberately hurt their children or spouses?

Ninety-nine percent of the time, these souls have absolutely nothing to feel guilty about. And if they do find something (clearly, something not very memorable if we had to work through a session or two to find it), I ask them to apply the principle regardless. Gaining perspective about weaknesses or mistakes and then releasing feelings of shame and guilt is the equivalent of pumping oxygen into a collapsed mine. The sense of entrapment is lifted, and suddenly and increasingly there is light at the end of the complex of relational tunnels.

Pandemic Guilt

Everyone who is mentally healthy has, at some time, done something about which he feels embarrassed or ashamed. These feelings are part and parcel of growing, learning, and maturing—indeed, to an extent, of being healthily, passionately human. Even when a patient tells me that he has done something so serious that even I, as a psychotherapist, must suppress an inclination to cringe, what has to be done is still clear. The individual needs an opportunity to air the issue. He needs to discuss the circumstances and people surrounding the incident, as well as what compelled him to do or say what he did, at that time and with the knowledge he had then.

We all need to do that occasionally throughout our lives. Further, we need to view our misactions from a less subjectively rigid perspective. We need, for example, to ask ourselves how we would judge a beloved sister, uncle, or best friend were she or he struggling with self-forgiveness related to the same issue. Invariably, where someone else is concerned, the guilt seems less necessary, even silly—and most definitely a waste of otherwise productive energy.

We are all exponentially more forgiving of others' actions than we are of our own. Whenever I have worked with someone and her guilt issues, she has been able to explain and accept the behavior when she imagined someone else performing it. Wallowing in our own guilt, we give ourselves life sentences, when three days probation would more than suffice. And this emotional imprisonment affects every aspect of our lives—especially our ability to love maturely, to be a living expression of our uniqueness, and to create.

Fallibility, Perfection, and Forgiveness

Clearly, we have to accept our own fallibility before we can forgive ourselves. Those of us who are perfectionists have probably never *not* felt guilty. Nothing perfectionists do is ever good enough—or just enough. In fact, driven perfectionists have an enormous load of visceral work precisely because of their guilt and anger about always having to be perfect.

The mandate to be perfect has undoubtedly been programmed since childhood and is intensely rooted in the stretched-tight fiber of a frenetic, conditional existence. Consequently, the Perfection Program is one of the most difficult to overcome.

It is also among the deadliest of self-destructive approaches to life. Perfectionists are falling like flies at a time when there is proof positive that there is no "perfect" in any human endeavor—the manufacture of a car, the writing of a term paper, an involvement in a corporate project, or even parenting. Left-brain, logical strivings for perfection get us nowhere in today's environment, yet they used to get us A-pluses. It is a hard lesson to learn: mere effort, even self-destructive do-it, do-it, and do-it-again effort, is, more often than not, futile in circumstances that require not just effort but creative risk-taking. A perfectionist or guilt-ridden person avoids risk as if it were cyanide! Being creative means that something might be done wrong or imperfectly or only half a step toward ordered completion—states of imperfection and incompleteness unbearable to the perfectionist.

Actual Self-Forgiving

No one needs to live with crippling guilt. It is not an easy state to overcome, but there are some practical steps that we can take in order to engage in a process leading to the loosening of forgiveness.

We can cut short our life sentences by merely taking the time to understand our behavior, by considering it as if someone else dear to us had committed the "unpardonable" act. Further, we can ascertain what it is that we feel guilty about and break it down into its basic components. When did we feel shamed, humiliated, or caught in badness? When were we condemned? Or did we condemn ourselves to a life of punitive, emotional paucity?

The answers to these questions are invariably irrational and illogical, but the process is still clarifying. It is also usually painful. Some grieving is required when we realize that we once decided (or let someone else decide) that we were guilty of something and that both the sentence and the sense of diminishment have stayed with us. However, it is also immeasurably freeing to put self-condemnation through the rationality test. It is liberating to find that we can stop the madness of self-imprisonment precisely because we ourselves have been carrying the secret program for self-recrimination. No external force or person has been teaching us anything about ourselves for years. Forgiving—or not forgiving—ourselves is now an inside job.

Even the perfectionist can and must force away the constant companion of guilt. Otherwise, in addition to self-destruction, perfectionists hurt, sometimes even destroy, their friends, family members, and coworkers by making impossible demands on them. Associates and relations, instantly intimidated, become increasingly displeased with themselves and endure new or intensified feelings of inadequacy and rejection.

Projected Guilt

As human individuals, we have the disastrous ability to project our own feelings of guilt or self-hatred onto others. If we are feeling guilty about something, it is par for human behavior to go on the offensive or to try to hand the emotion to someone nearby—a supervisor, a spouse, even a child of the family. Further, if we live with unmanaged feelings of guilt, we become guilt magnets. If it is around us, we will attract it and further self-define and condemn ourselves.

It is absolutely critical, therefore, that we examine our own feelings of specific or general culpability in order to avoid taking on or making something out of the guilt feelings of those around us. Indeed, although much projection is inadvertent, part of the complex workings of the human subconscious, some is tactical. We find ourselves sinking deeper and deeper into a thick, sticky morass of guilt as a result of the behavior of someone else in our lives. In that we felt guilty to begin with (something the other person no doubt picked up on immediately), we are open to accepting new levels and varieties of self-condemnation with the systematic assistance of our associates or partners in shame.

The cruelest human games are played with guilt at the center. And guilt stifles all that is loving and extraordinary about the human animal. If we find that our lives are being restricted by feelings of guilt and general unforgivability, we must dare to speak these feelings, first to ourselves and then to an empathetic, intelligent, and outspoken friend, relative, or life partner. We are well served by sharing these restricting feelings with someone (as long as he or she is our protector, not our projector) and then returning to and having a chat with our inner Selves—the part of us that has been doing penance for what is likely no more than growing up. Then we have to listen to our thoughts and the complex emotionality around our selves and our behavior in all our environments. Further and just as important, we have to open our hearts to the guiding insights that come to us from a place of detached silence.

Self-Trust, Pride, and Forgiveness

George Bernard Shaw wrote that he could not "abide those who are virtuous but mean in word and deed." We find it extremely difficult to accept that bad things can happen to good people *and* that good people can do bad things. Frequently, the perpetrators are unaware of the fact that they have left hordes of people wounded and wondering, even into old age, why they were attacked, rejected, or suddenly ignored.

Thus, the absence of self-forgiveness, irrationally related to the misactions and injuries perpetrated upon us by others, is a deep, dark, and intensely personal posture. Each of us, at some time or another, has been deeply hurt, even damaged, by other human beings whom we thought were friends or good folk incapable of cruelty. Yet it is often easier to blame ourselves than to challenge our basic black-and-white illusions about human behavior.

Indeed, it is common, even normal psychological behavior for the victims of cruelty or misaction to feel guilty themselves. We may wait years for apologies or explanations that never come, all the while wondering what we did to provoke the loss. The attacker gets absolved because of our innate sense of overresponsibility and our need to believe in the goodness of others.

Moreover, because of basic human fear, historic guilt, and universal pride, very few of us who are hurt find the courage to risk the indignity of just asking the perpetrator why the attack, misaction, or rejection occurred. Like pathetic prey to a schoolyard bully, most of us are significantly more likely to tiptoe off in pain, with another layer of self-condemnation added to our already brittle hearts.

And the damage goes on and on, precisely because we are more likely to hide and lick our wounds than we are to make fundamental behavioral demands of each other as adults.

Banal Atrocities—Not a Game Show

Thus, we are well served by finding the courage to look at the most painful, difficult, and common forms of attack to which we subject each other and around which there is the greatest need for forgiveness. The issues are, generally speaking, related to manipulative dishonesty, misrepresentation of someone to others, and seemingly arbitrary abandonment.

Regardless of the apparent poise and pseudo-calm of many people, most really do not know how they would react in different circumstances and have not cared to find out. Thus, these apparently virtuous people cannot be trusted on a fundamental level or counted on to be consistent under all circumstances, especially in crisis.

The former statement is a serious one, and I do not write it lightly. However, it is a truth that causes too much damage to be left unstated or couched in obfuscating language. Seemingly good people with specific weaknesses or actual destructive agendas can come into our lives and wreak havoc with our hearts, reputations, and finances. Many failed marriages, precipitously terminated friendships, and ruthlessly severed business arrangements have ended this way, leaving both parties diminished, both reputations tarnished, and at least one victim in a destructive state of embaffled loss. The confusion and potential for a new level of shame and guilt is one of the irresponsible handoffs left from the misactions of the cruelly self-ignorant.

Shame, Self-Blame, and Forgiveness

Unfortunately, too many fine souls can identify with being on the receiving end of the generic misactions just mentioned. Further, as already implied, too many people turn the atrocities of others back upon themselves. When we are shocked by what seems to be the precipitously negative behavior of others, many of us reflexively examine *ourselves* for culpability, rather than try to understand the misbehavior of the perpetrators. Over and over again, we rethink our own statements or behavior to ascertain how we might be responsible for someone else's actions. After all, we have our self-forgiveness issues to contend with, and if we are among the majority, we are still on emotional parole. Consequently, many of us first blame ourselves, rather than someone we have cared for and trusted.

Blame itself is not really the issue. But we have to get past irrational self-blame in order to rationally assess the misactions of others, especially the cruelties of someone we have allowed to be close to us. When we have decided to risk letting someone know us, we have accepted that person's apparent strengths and weaknesses in a somewhat idealized form. It is easy, therefore, to understand why we irrationally search within ourselves for some explanation of the change of behavior in someone to whom we had given ourselves in trust. It behooves us to do so precisely because we made a judgment call to let someone close enough to hurt us.

The reflex is a way of saving face with ourselves. Indeed, in addition to our hurt feelings and confusion, we have to deal with our damaged pride. Part of the shame and self-blame is directly related to fundamental questions that we now have to ask ourselves about the soundness of our judgment. And this inner shakedown is extremely painful and disconcerting. Consequently, we prefer to find something concrete about ourselves, our actions, or our behavior—a clear cause and effect—to explain why we were attacked and implicitly rejected.

Fascinatingly if heart-renderingly, as vulnerable, tentatively loving beings, we would rather be guilty of some misaction than have been wrong in our judgment of someone we had come to love and trust. It is much more difficult to have to admit that people in our lives can misact, can be downright mean, insensitive, and uncaring about our feelings. It is emotionally eviscerating to realize that we no longer have (or never did have) the honest respect of someone for whom we have cared. Reflexively, we choose shame and self-blame over condemnation (and total loss) of a companion-become-culprit. It is easier to search for, find (usually by fabrication), and admit to error than it is to accept the apparent fact of our eminent lack of worth and rejectability.

What an enormous task it is for us to see beyond our own inveterate self-doubt to the reality that many, if not most people are (to use the language of my theology) lost—that is, either unaware of or uncaring about how their actions affect others.

The same majority misses out on the joy inherent in affecting others in positive ways, small and large, one of the myriad benefits of conscious living, as opposed to lost, benumbed, and selfish unconscious living. However, to live consciously and "response-ably" is also to recognize the potentially damaging teeth of this distinctly human interactive conundrum. It is a fact that people who once claimed to love or otherwise value us can, with cold pragmatism and private, precipitous agendas that have nothing to do with us, hurt us and, in effect, reject us. It happens daily to thousands of individual hearts.

Yet it is understandable that, without the benefit and salvation of comprehension, we are inclined to just wander off in shame. Where complex, interactive issues are concerned, we, as a species, have not changed in thousands of years, except that, many argue, we have become more numbly pragmatic about committing injurious behavior.

The walking wounded among us are innumerable. Many of us suffer feelings of inferiority, rejection, and a fearful, attenuated distrust of ourselves and our own judgment. And although conscious living requires that we take responsibility where responsibility should be taken, we too often victimize ourselves as a result of the misactions of others. Further and unfortunately, some people have a conscious handle on manipulating this common human fallibility, a not uncommon emotional disorder. Suffice it to say that in combating and controlling their own demons, a potent minority of human players exploit others with what appears to be a complete absence of empathy or mercy.

Shame, the Preemptor of Active Forgiveness

Less-evolved humans knew a trick thousands of years ago, before the magnificent, analytic redundancies of modern psychology and psychoanalysis. It was called *shunning*. When conflict arose within a tribe or village, the individual with whom others were displeased would be left without explanation (or empathy, understanding, or corrective instruction) and then abandoned. Guilty and shamed, that individual would meekly accept the tacit ruling without benefit of a trial or discussion. Soon after, he would wander, exiled from his home, family, and friends, with what even scientists would refer to as a broken heart, of which he would usually die, remarkably quickly.

The modern form of shunning is exclusionary violence, and when we are its victims, we are, fortunately albeit absurdly, too busy and too laden with too many responsibilities to die. We just keep living with more self-doubt and with increasingly and perilously wounded souls. And eventually, we die sooner than we should. Modern shunning, the result of projected and accepted blame turned to guilt and humiliation, is the precursor to at least half a dozen fatal diseases. Holding on to the pain brought on by the misactions of uncaring others can literally kill us because the pain is aimed at and carried by us, not the perpetrator. Shame maims.

Ironically, modern society has honed technologies that, although meant to bring us together (to do business, of course, not just to connect interpersonally), actually make this primitive practice of exclusionary violence easier and more pointed. Now, we can code people out of our lives and be decoded out of others on an irrational whim or in an over-reactive moment.

Look how far we have come! We still have to learn to understand complex primitive behavior. But that behavior, fundamentally unchanged, is now driven by individual and global technologies that enhance our ability to damage and destroy. I know of no scientist willing to predict when we may be sufficiently grown up as human beings to use our technologies to love—or even when and under what critical circumstances we may find ourselves inclined to do so. We are subsumed in a high-tech rat race to keep abreast of changing technology, when we should be relearning the basic tactile dimensions of our most primitive relationships.

We give in to modern shunning, to shame and guilt, when we choose to avoid the difficult process of face-to-face, active forgiveness. We are trying to live in a society that pays little more than lip service to resolution and understanding. Consequently, the control of forgiveness is, more often than not, in the hands of the perpetrator. Very few victims will attempt to discuss cruel behavior for fear of being further hurt. Very few witnesses to such behavior will call disapproving attention to it lest they be hit in the line of fire. The majority of us tend toward denial, polite silence, and acquiescence when we witness nefarious behavior. The remaining minority are litigious and primed for battle; not surprisingly, they are frequently instigators of conflict themselves.

Forgiveness: An Ongoing Journey

The best that we can do, in the face of actions that are incomprehensibly hurtful, is to try to emit, consistently and *selfishly*, the light and love of forgiveness. The key comes in the form of understanding, self-knowledge, and, most important, self-trust.

In order to work at forgiveness in the case of losses, small or great, we have to work on the belief that the individuals involved have no idea how much pain they have caused us or that they do know but cannot consciously confront their own mental or emotional challenges. The most useful approach is to perceive our attackers as (in the language of my theology) lost and inept, rather than bad or evil. Most people who attack and injure others have profound, unconscious fears, as well as an inability to forgive themselves for previous mistakes or misactions. Further, they are often people who have not done any work toward forgiving those who caused them the hurts and injustices of childhood. Consequently, they cannot accept or forgive *anyone*. To them, others frequently mirror unforgiven people from their pasts. They are basically, if unnecessarily, inadequate individuals who trust no one but their families (and sometimes not even them). Further, lacking trust or real self-confidence, they are often impulsive, self-contradictory, and reflexively dishonest. Initially, they exude charm and sweetness to the core. But they perceive and react to even minor errors as if they were life-threatening attacks. This lost—and dangerous—personality type is too common, and commonly sad.

Unfortunately, therefore, even if we can face the daunting challenge of attempting active forgiveness and openly and vulnerably communicate our queries, it often becomes apparent that the perpetrator herself is both unapproachable and unforgiving. Because of her angry, internal protective intransigence, she cannot listen to or accept attempts at resolution. In this shaky, Humpty Dumpty world, those without empathy or conscience do their pragmatic deeds. Their precariously disordered characters control whatever they can and eliminate what gets in their way. Yet only when these people manifest themselves in actual physical violence is the real source of shame addressed and relieved—by firm institutional understanding and containment.

Merely Respectable Living

Actively (or passively) attempting to make sense out of the painful behavior of others is not especially heroic. It is merely the only way to unshackle ourselves from an impossibly complex morass of life's hurts and betrayals. The ultimate gift to the other person notwithstanding, such action should be an automatic, ongoing part of the process of sane living as a human with other humans. It should not be escapable or avoidable. Misbehavior among adults who know better will continue. Indeed, many social scientists and futurists believe such behavior will soon predominate. All the more reason to include the practice of forgiveness, overt or covert, as part of the short and already arduous, lesson-filled journey from birth to death.

Commonality

Most of us experienced the pain and confusion of inexplicable loss or rejection, the overlapping consequences of cruel or thoughtless behavior in grade school and have known it since several if not many times. It is such a common experience at all ages that someone should start support groups for the precipitously rejected or injured!

What differentiates human beings from other animals is our ability to think logically, to communicate, and to empathize. Yet too many of us are able to suspend or have let atrophy skills in these key behavioral areas. It is a frightening fact that we can, despite the enormous capacities of the human heart, slam the door on other hearts. To close one's heart on another is, to all and any of us, an attack on the soul. It removes both the precious, life-giving presumption of love and friendship from the victim and love from the life of the individual who does the slamming. To do so without explanation is to induce madness-like confusion, not to mention pain, in a fellow human being who undoubtedly already suffers at least an average dose of guilt and regret.

Interestingly, the psychological literature and private practitioners like myself find that people have more problems related to rejection and loss than to any other issue. And these problems are among the most difficult to overcome, to process through to a posture of forgiveness. Given the innate and infinitely profound human need for acceptance, issues related to divorce, the death of a parent, and other forms of loss are both life-stingers and life-stiflers. They tend to stick within an individual because of the complexity of the feelings involved, including humiliation and self-blame.

For the same reasons, however, these issues are among the most important for us to resolve, with or without the involvement of the lost party or parties. Loss issues scream for the need to learn to forgive both oneself and others. Forgiveness is not merely a nice thing to do—it is a lifestyle choice with life and death ramifications.

A Difficult Process

If forgiving were easy, or, in fact, if we really understood its nature, process, and benefits, we would be less likely to hurt ourselves by holding onto anger, vengefulness, or attenuated humiliation. But letting go is not easy. Of course, if a damaging or hurtful incident can be discussed and resolved, what is needed is more understanding than forgiveness. Forgiving should be easy when someone explains his actions and apologizes. It is another thing altogether when there will never be a chance to review or resolve the issue with the person or persons involved.

This is the challenge of forgiveness. It is a process that involves ridding ourselves of anger and finding a place of inner peace with ourselves and the person in apparent need of forgiveness. The process also requires that we move forward with a sadness that goes away only with time and with increased understanding and wisdom. We have really forgiven when we no longer feel that there is anything to forgive. Only then are those involved in the life lesson truly free of both the lesson and the unhealthy interconnection.

An Object Lesson?

Most of the time, most human beings are either unaware of or unthinking about what they are doing. Because we leave our thoughts and actions unexamined, some of us are unconscious of the fact that we have virtually mutilated another human heart. Although one can argue that this distinctively human "dumbness" has always defined the majority of people, there is no doubt that as we have "advanced" socially and techno-logically, we have increased the emotional and perceptual distance be-tween individuals. Self-knowledge and, therefore, self-responsibility are not requisites, either educationally or socially, in a society ruled by the buck. Mutual care and responsibility are frighteningly rare preoccupations of a frighteningly small minority of people. With our ostensible advance-ment has come *anomie,* a word Émile Durkheim, a founder of sociology, used to denote the alienation and unfeelingness of fast-paced, market-driven relations in the 19th century. Pertinently, he describes anomie and its foundational analysis in his most famous book, which is titled *Suicide.*

Now, the "me" decade of the 1980s has turned into the "massacre" pe-riod of the 1990s and the millennium. Studies show that we *are* growing meaner (defensive and frightened) and, in many ways, less capable of empathy.

If I hurt you, it should hurt me. Yet when many people hear that proposition, they stare blankly, uncomprehending of why someone else's pain should affect them in any way. They just don't get it—or, more im-portant, feel it.

The myriad scary ramifications of this common condition aside, it is one more reason why ostensibly good people hurt other good people. In this time-challenged life we lead, too many of us have stopped caring (or no longer have the energy to care) about the effect we have on others. Some social scientists suggest that, from an inverted Darwinian per-spective, we are mutating backwards, devolving into benumbed androids, manically performing with an intense commitment to self and lifestyle, rather than to each other and to life.

The bottom line is that some people do not mean to be destructive or hurtful. Even with the unconsciously nasty, however, too often face-to-face resolution or mutual discussion of conflict is impossible. Those who have lost heart, empathy, and a sense of connectedness with others have no inner contract with the real emotional rhythms of life. They expedite their days and weeks according to a rabid, self-centered prag-matism that, to them, feels like survival and precarious success. Many *do* know, on one level, what they have done, but they can't afford to know and care. So they just don't.

The Forgiveness Litmus Test

If we can forgive the unexplainable, the unresolved, and the seemingly un-provoked cruelty of those who hurt and run, we are true forgivers. And significant benefits accrue to those of us who can forgive. We are healthier, happier, more understanding and open, and more creative as thinking and loving beings.

As forgivers, we are also infinitely less likely to cause pain. First, we feel and understand pain too well ourselves to inflict it. Second, we are without the reflexively condemning (and perceptually contorting) baggage that comes with holding on to enemies from the past. To forgivers, the overused word *hate* is the most obscene four-letter word in the English language. It gives constant subliminal permission to exclude, attack, and walk away from battered or broken souls.

The Gift of Forgiveness

Leo Tolstoy wrote that the most selfish act of his life was to forgive his father for apparently alternately abusing and ignoring him. I, too, consider the time that I have taken to work to forgive several people in my life to have been quality time *selfishly* spent. I did not want to live with the pain and anger associated with feeling "wrong done by" by those who abandoned me as an infant or wounded me as a fledgling adult. The best thing for me was to speak with them (whether or not they were alive or accessible to me), come to understand the ways in which *they* were lost (struggling, afraid, and confused) when they hurt me, and then try to come to accept them.

What a magnificent light and lightness the process of forgiving can bring us. Refusing to forgive allows us to make more excuses and to stall in all aspects of our lives because we deem ourselves damaged goods. What muted darkness many of us live in because we cannot—or choose not to—forgive. The inability to forgive is a ball and chain that makes our lives mere dutiful drags. We can live in no way other than disheartened, disconnected, and, inevitably, mean subsistence.

Indeed, the greatest gain from forgiveness accrues to the forgiver. Yet those who are forgiven unquestionably benefit, whether they consciously know it or not. They are affected by the change in our energetic perspectives toward them, and in time, unless they are disordered, their energy invariably changes toward us. Ironically, the best thing that we can do with respect to either the resolvable or the unresolvable, after whatever action is possible, is to change how the action is positioned in our inner world. This way, loss or a perceived attack can take on a new, minimized, and less-polluting place in our psyches.

How

Once, in Dallas, Texas, just after I had given a lecture on the role that forgiveness plays in our private and work lives, three members of the audience waited in line to ask me "how?" I thought to myself, "What time does my flight leave? Do I have a week?" The "how" of forgiveness, beyond the blunt instruction either to try to understand or to let go of the incomprehensible, is really the essence of the act. It involves committing ourselves to a primarily internal process of reliving and redoing the original action and, by so doing, rescripting the scenario and those in it. In addition, it involves and requires daily auto-suggestive work in which we imagine ourselves articulating our forgiveness to the person or persons involved. To complete the psychic-emotional cycle, we need to imagine the heartful acceptance of our sentiments as well as the warm articulation of an explanation on the part of the person who hurt us.

Critically, we must speak only positively of that person. We must commit ourselves to this action because what we say, we come to believe, thus soothing our hearts and releasing ourselves from anger. (The alternative perpetuates our inner tension by building on negativity.) It is also, of course, the right thing to do and distinguishes us from those who cannot, yet or ever, live in kind, fearless consciousness of others.

In short, to stay in a place of anger and remain vengeful is to remain in a petrified emotional trap. It also ensures that we will continue to emit energy that feeds the ill will of our ostensible enemies and perhaps even attracts the ill will of others. Almost as frequently as the actively uncaring, those who are passively vengeful become perpetrators of pain.

Choice

Fortunately, our subconscious minds are such that they do not know the difference between an experience in "real" life and one we have scripted and simulated in a state of rest and quiet. With the latter kind of experience done repeatedly (for some, just once), we can both forgive and release the anger and grief related to old and new injuries and perceived injustices.

This result will come, assuming, of course, that we really want to benefit from forgiving and that we do not have the all-too-common need to remain angry or in adversary. Too many of us avoid the practical process of forgiving because anger and divisiveness provide a vibrant, "filling" familiarity. Moreover, forgiving is hard work, requiring a commitment to change and self-development in a society that puts little stock in inner development and perhaps even less in diminishing what is considered the normative, conflict-driven order of things. In short, there is little encouragement for inner work, let alone for forgiving those who have hurt us. People love a good, sustained fight. Long-term feuds have great entertainment value for those who are seduced by the allure of conflict. (Further complicate conflict with a conspiracy theory, and virtually everyone wants to be your friend.)

The how of forgiveness is, in large part, wanting to forgive and committing ourselves to doing so as part of who we are (without, of course, becoming doormats). We should practice forgiveness every day, on small levels, over small incidents. We should also, as mentioned earlier, meditate—think and focus—on active forgiveness in an auto-suggestive or deeply relaxed state of neutrality and stillness.

Remember that we can rescript a part of our lives *only* if we want to, choose to, and commit ourselves to the work required. We also have to be powerfully self-motivated in a world that both enjoys and perpetuates conflict as a norm. Therefore, those of us who think, feel, and choose to live with as much peace as possible must have the determination, courage, and the resilience to stay that way.

Ironically, one of the ways in which we can strengthen our hearts and our resolve is to choose daily someone to forgive and to process that gift at the level of heart. By so doing, we learn that forgiveness is, first and foremost, a gift to ourselves and then a gift to the other person. Thus, at least two people, usually more, come significantly closer to being healed from the violent ramifications of either malevolence or mere thoughtlessness.

Forgiveness is the F word that stands for the undoing and healing of violations between and among what are usually equally needy souls. It is a distinctly, beatifically human gift. It is also a tonic with universal applications in environments characterized by increasingly complex and intense human relations.

CASE STUDY

Robert Forgives His Father and Himself

Robert's wife insisted that he get therapy. In fact, she pushed the issue because she felt that something was keeping him from rising faster in the technology firm in which he was a young middle manager. In fact something *was* blocking his progress, but he couldn't talk to his wife about it. The problem was longstanding: his father's rejection of him.

Robert had aspired to a white-collar career, while his father, Emilio, was a blue-collar worker. Although Robert wanted his parents to be proud of him, his father wasn't. Rather, the older man felt that Robert was spurning his way of life—that his son wanted to be better than his father. As a result, no matter what Robert did, Emilio saw it as an insult or a reflection of his own inadequacy. The father would not attend any of Robert's graduations, didn't care where he worked, and did not show any semblance of interest in what he did. Soon into Robert's career, the two men stopped talking altogether.

Around the time Emilio died, Robert began to self-sabotage at work, to show less interest, and to avoid opportunities for promotion. His wife, a highly ambitious woman, eventually told him to get help or get out of the marriage.

In our first therapy session, it became evident that Robert felt painfully guilty about never having made up with his father—indeed, that he had never told him that he loved him. He also felt that he had been a disappointment to his father and that he would never be forgiven by this man, whom he basically loved.

In our third session together, we did a hypnotic exercise in which we had Robert "meet" his father on the bank of a river where they once fished together when Robert was a child. Built into the hypnotic experience were both fishing and talking. Essentially, we had Robert tell his father how he felt, how he needed his pride, and how he sought his forgiveness if he had inadvertently hurt him. We also had Emilio tell Robert that he loved him, that he was proud of his son, and that there was nothing to forgive. They then spent much time holding each other, weeping joyfully by the water.

When Robert emerged from the hypnotic state, he wept some more. The resolution of such a fundamental part of his life seemed miraculous to him. But no miracle was involved. Robert had experienced the expressions of mutual love and forgiveness just as if he had actually been with his living father. To the subconscious mind, everything experienced at a depth of relaxation and focus is as real as *real*.

Robert proceeded to soar in his company but with less stress and strain than before. To this day, he feels that his hypnotic session was the most meaningful time of his life. And no one can convince him that he did not see, speak to, and resolve things with his father. In terms of reconnecting and redoing the relationship, he did have this healing time with Emilio. Robert experienced and shared forgiveness at a level of mind that is at least as powerful as a full waking state.

EXERCISE

Forgive yourself and others today, and reduce the mental, emotional and physical stress that come with gripped anger. Make a practice of forgiving someone, in your mind, each night before going to sleep.

Also, practice one aspect of conscious living. Determine how your actions have affected and do affect others. If you think that you have hurt someone, ask her. If you know you have, find the courage to approach her and replace pain and simmering conflict with understanding, shared relief, and peace. Note the effect of understanding and forgiveness on your own heart, let alone the effect that your responsible actions have on your loved one, friend, or associate.

Principle 3

Fear: A Four-Letter Word

Recognize your own fears, observe yourself with others, and admit that you are unnecessarily fearful—even if some people have given you reason to be. Health, healing, and the ability to love, even to be successful at whatever you are and do are only available to those who let go of fear.

All that a universally benevolent deity would ask of us in order to ensure that our prayers and dreams come true is that we not live in and with fear.

John Randolph Price

Too many of us struggle with fear, and much of the fear that we matter-of-factly carry through life is related to the principles discussed in these pages. For example, we are fearful of people we cannot forgive. One reason for our reluctance to let go of our anger and to forgive is a need to remain tensely vigilant for reattack. Our egos remain on the alert, injured but tight-fisted for the next round with the same person or group or with someone new. Fearful living and the anticipation of attack have virtually become epidemic.

A second reason for living in a state of fear is not having learned to accept and to be comfortable with who we are. We are constantly fearful of being "found out," of being revealed as the inadequate, even guilty beings we believe that we are. Most of us feel that we are lucky to be accepted, to have a good job, even to have found a good mate. Moreover, in that we feel lucky, which implies undeserving, we are ever fearful of losing what we have fortuitously acquired. This fear translates into gripping behavior that does nothing but ensure that people will move away from or be lost to us, if not literally, then in some other way.

All too many of us are also fearful of life itself. In an era when work-related risk-taking is value-added, a person who fears life can bring little value to job or career and has little security in the way of employability. Fear is stifling, paralyzing, and allows for nothing new under the protective yet precarious roof of luck. With this affliction, we cannot *really* risk loving, really risk self-examination, or really risk working toward self-expression. Rather, we remain guardedly, self-protectively mute and immobilizingly agreeable. Fearful people do not make waves—even good ones. They keep the waters calm at all cost.

Fearfulness Is Toxic

Another key aspect of fearful living is that we are unable to risk holding opinions, particularly controversial ones. We are unable to step in where the actions of others are destructive or to question the unfair or unjust criticisms, even the outright cruelty of others. We duck and let things ride in order to remain ostensibly comfortable, assuming that our self-betrayal wreaks no external or unconscious damage. Fearful, we cannot do the adult thing: honor ourselves and others. Even on a good day, the fearful among us dare not laugh too loudly for fear of drawing attention to ourselves and thus suffering a mild degree of scrutiny. Unless we have positioned ourselves to exert petty power, we keep our mouths and hearts shut and our heads down. And then maybe, we hope, we will not become a target for the latest office or neighborhood bully.

Worth mentioning is a common but especially toxic form of fearful malexistence. Unlike the fearful adult who keeps her mouth shut and head down, essentially minding her own business, some fearful people seek protective vantage by speaking ill of others. They take on what is virtually the role of an informer, passing on bits and pieces of real, imaginary, or half-true information to someone they deem to be in a position to make or break them and others.

Extremely common in traditional office situations, this behavior is also, ironically, classic sibling behavior. That we emulate childhood roles in our adult life at work should be no surprise. Those who fed the authority figure in their homes as children often, with compounded insecurity, do so later as adult employees and managers.

What is tragic about this seemingly harmless need to pass on the goods regarding another person (essentially, gossiping with intent) is that the informer, seemingly innocent, is actually feeding the need of a controller to stay one step ahead of what he fears in the way of an unforseen, uncontrolled problem, major or minor. There exists, therefore, a codependent relationship between the fearful informer and the fearful controller, even if, as is usually the case, the controller has little respect for the informer. In fact, little does the informer know that she has placed herself in a highly insecure position with the person she so diligently but destructively serves. Ultimately, the price paid for such dubious service is active contempt.

The behavior just described is a major fear-spreader in small organizations and in divisions within large ones. When I am asked to assess a morale problem in an office environment or to investigate "problem employees," something similar to this phenomenon is invariably at work. Good employees can feel nervous and baffled when they pick up subtle indicators that something is afoot around them. Of course, the mature employee investigates, asks questions of a supervisor, or in some other way attempts to clarify and discard the disturbing sense that something is not quite right. In an environment that condones the informer-controller dyad, however, there can be no truth or clarity. The fearful informer tells the fearful controller what he wants to hear or what she wants him to hear, and all other communication is cut off, distorted, or tainted by this poisonous mix of fearful reportage and complex, personal agendas.

This scenario is by far the most efficient way to create a toxic environment in the workplace. Each employee, associate, even customer is affected in some way by the mixed messages and twisted layers of miscommunication. For the employees, it is the fastest way to induce confusion and lethargy—the consequences of the absence of a sense of openness and clarity. People will not commit themselves to an environment or to a task when the activity around them is defined by secrets, deniable malevolence, and subversive control. The dyad (sometimes a competitive triad), touches everyone who enters or deals with the environment. It is deadly for performance, trust, and basic goodwill.

Fear Begets Fear

As already implied, fear spreads like wildfire. Given our ability to store, access, react to, and reenact historic fears, we are easily set off by even the most elementary manipulations of other fearful beings. Given our propensity for fear, we feel, use, and abuse it with each other in myriad ways. Some are conscious and some unconscious, but none is an attribute of those who are committed to conscious living.

One of the major problems is that fear itself, as a state, is mutually compelling, particularly where competition still triumphs over cooperation and other kinds of mutually supportive conduct. Mammals are attracted to fear in other mammals, and human beings are no exception. If we live unconsciously, we are unaware of how much fear we are communicating, not to mention in what way and to what degree we react to fear in others. In short, most of us do not deal with this mutually attracting state either in the way we should, were we empathetic, caring beings, or in the way we could if we were to take time to learn about, review, and change our behavior.

As in our childhood (and increasingly, studies show, in today's schoolyards and playgrounds), there is a bully in every environment. In ostensible adulthood, the bullies are often those who were bullied, not the bulliers, in their early years. In conscious or unconscious payback mode, they precipitate conflict and discomfort among those they feel they can trick or manipulate into fear states. Like child bullies, they can sniff out the most fearful or self-questioning in any group within days. Studies show, for example, that an office bully (especially one who espouses all the right words but spurns new-era concepts in her actions) will almost immediately connect with vulnerable colleagues or associates who are perfectionists. It is clear to the office bully, on a basic animal level, that a driven perfectionist is actually fearful, self-doubting, and self-punitive, in spite of his obvious competencies.

Indeed, perfectionists are fear magnets: they attract the bully's fear, which is translated into what is often insidiously manipulative aggression. The adult bully is acting out her own feelings of fear and inadequacy with the perfect partner in fear—the hardworking, self-demanding, yet insecure perfectionist. The perfectionist's fear draws the underlying fear of the bully to himself like bees to nectar.

The old saying is that misery loves company. So does the misery of fear. It is an attraction based on cruelty, and it is downright inexcusable when it is played out among or between adults. Fear, however, transcends both espoused ethics and chronological maturity.

Ours Is the Fear Era

The times are strange, virtually surreal. We live in *Star Trek* with apparent (if easily defeated) convictions pertinent to *Little House on the Prairie*. With a profound and unaddressed fear of rapid change compounded by a bland and blind acceptance of sterility in much of our lives, including the denuding absence of basic privacy, we see and are exposed to everything but feel very little of the pain of our fellow humans. Although we are shocked for at least an hour after hearing that elementary school children are so badly behaved that they shoot each other, we all share an ineffable sense of how far beyond real peaceful coexistence we have already gone.

In fairness, if we were to react appropriately to every atrocity we view or hear about in a day, we would die of instant heartbreak, of sheer disgust, or of downright terror. However, we don't. With so much done for us and with so much homey technology to protect us, we go through our earning years accumulating but unconsciously yearning for impossible connections. And while we live with suppressed yearning and barely repressed fear, we commit unpardonable acts of ignorance and pragmatic cruelty.

An Example

A defining anomaly of the fear era, an incident-become-world-event worth much personal reflection, took place while I was writing this book. The sudden, tragic death of Diana Spencer was, among other things, a fascinating shared catharsis.

A perfect example of an extraordinary celebrity whose life overflowed with pathos, the princess struggled with banalities such as fear, loss, self-hatred, hope, and a will to contribute and to self-define, all the while oozing pathological insecurity. Her mundanely tragic death terrified and moved us all.

Even before her death, she had personified our struggles, our unarticulated fears, our guilt, our self-doubt, and our will toward personal significance, and many of us apotheosized her for so doing. We had what Emily Bird, a notable anthropologist, refers to as a "parasocial relationship" with this young woman, so she had become an icon by and at the point of her impossible death.

She was, before we knew it, a peripheral but daily living symbol of our own needs and neediness. The relationship, intensely intimate but one-sided, was played out, taken for granted, and then snatched from us in a way that revealed much that is terribly sad about us. We felt that we knew her. With her failings and frills, she represented an artificially intimate constant in what is, for too many of us, an empty, dreamless, drab existence. As wounded beauty, she was assumed to be immortal, a forever-living symbol touching us with her latest (literally) touching commitment to the identifiable and ostensibly controversial. She could make a difference, where we could not—or would dare not try. And in her death, she reminded us of our eminent vulnerability.

Among the many pathetically human attributes we shared with Lady Di was the banal fact that most of us enjoy driving too fast but never expect to crash. She was not supposed to have died this way, to have brought this gross tragedy to our relationship with her. We mourned as a half-us, half-deflecting fairy tale, perhaps the last one ever, ended in a mangled mess—a ghastly way to lose the protection of projection.

The attenuated, paralyzing mourning was (her children aside) for ourselves. In our own fearful conformity, we had been able to hide and to transfer our deepest repressions to her. We had been able to sublimate our instinctive awareness of the fact that without an absence of fear and without true meaning in our lives, we are mere bugs on a windshield.

This very public sufferer's death was a mighty shake-up, a catharsis for the greater part of the population of the western world. We could not explain why we felt the way we did: undone, as if we knew her (ourselves); angry (for what she and we had been through); and terrified that such an accident could happen (to us, to her), even in an armored car. Even money, which we worship as the source of salvation, could not repair the perfect young body. What about us?

A beautiful, objectified symbol of our secret fears and problems, she left us holding those parts of ourselves that we were projecting onto her so as to avoid facing them ourselves. There had to be a reaction. A huge one. The world had to participate in what was described within hours as an "unprecedented" and "inexplicable" mourning over the death of an internationally renowned figure. Our lives stopped (luckily, it was a Sunday: somehow, we could not hustle to prepare for a formal work week of ritualistic tasks). And with bashful ambivalence, we looked to others, to complete strangers, to share feelings that we could not yet accept or define.

Unlike the death of a world leader, this accident was not another dark lesson in the blurred layers of danger and madness amid which we live. Most of us had settled with the reality and probability of political violence years ago. This death pointed out something intensely personal, and we couldn't bear it. We participated in days of virtual "Di-ification" so that we could both freeze her lively ubiquity and adjust our projection. We needed to find a way—and we still can if we choose—to hide, to fuse with her in memory, and to position ourselves in her embellished legacy. We need to do this until we come upon another living symbol who is wealthy (the impoverished don't attract the press or our admiration), is suffering with apparent grace, is sufficiently lost and injured to act out our secret needs and desires, even our shame, and is photographed in a sufficiently excessive number of grim and beatified moments to enable us to identify with her.

The enormity of the irony in Diana's life and death, however, was and is, for the most part, lost to us. We were not even aware, until she was gone, that *she* was *us*.

Another Example

If we needed the clarity that comes with juxtaposition, we got it with Mother Teresa's death the same week. That death was somehow less startling and personal, though eerily coincidental.

This great woman, with the tranquility that comes with faith and certitude, had devoted her entire life, from age 36 (Lady Di's age at death), to good works, rejecting luxuries, personal financial reward, and press coverage (unless, of course, the latter benefited the helpless).

It is interesting, if not discomfiting, that we felt so differently about her passing, which was merely noted amid the near panic over the death of the suffering princess. Yet the difference shouldn't be surprising. In addition to Mother Teresa's being elderly and infirm, a condition that doesn't play well with any of us, she was so unlike us as to be impossible to identify with in life or in death. She was unafraid and sure of herself, her life, and her God. She was none of us in life. She wasn't living our broken dreams, hidden fears, and secret agendas, nor was she a symbol of our guilt. Ironically, we did not even ascribe heroism to this once-wealthy woman who, by choice, lived with and devoted every waking moment to human beings we wouldn't want to look at, let alone touch. Unintimidated though lauded by heads of state and endorsed by the crowning friendship and admiration of the Pope, she was just an exceptional old woman who died—in the same week and the wake of a princess. Sad but not a world stopper. Even sadder.

Our Own Reality

Of all inconvenient emotionality, the tidy and politically correct repression and projection of fear partially defines our fear era. Given how most of us have interpreted the new commandments of work and modern living, we don't dare *show* fear, confusion, or the secret, intolerable, epidemic condition of exhaustion. We hide it, our feelings, and ourselves in order to appear acceptable and valuable to the new order.

If the 1980s were slick, the current decade is downright buffed! We rub our edginess so as to shine above the crowd (as we were taught in grade school) or at least to stay within it. If the truth were shared, we would not be so potentially vicious or easily threatened by each other. We would each know that we are as fearful, as increasingly baffled, and as dull-wittedly fatigued as our neighbors and competitors—indeed, that those of us who are faking life, in fear, do so in fine and formidable company.

This peculiar era is also one whose apparent technological tidiness and efficiency has ironically left us more driven by primitive fears than at any time since World War II. With all apparently taken care of (including, we believe, the nuclear threat that riddled our nightmares as children), we have re-turned our fears on race in general and on each other and those who are different specifically. It is no consequence of judicial mishap that racism, notably against African-Americans in the United States, has soared back almost to the mood of the 1960s. It is also no coincidence that we merely listened with listless comfort to the debate as to whether to "take out" Saddam Hussein, the latest bad man in the global arena, along with families, schools, and hospitals. Saddam almost gave us something to talk about, a reason to pretend to share while debating outcomes and placing bets on body counts. We almost had something that we could pretend was more interesting, even more important than the sex life of the US president.

In reality, in the controlled, tight, and spiritually strangling existences of most middle-class Caucasian North Americans, we are so safe that we are terrified. And with no big enemy, even an artificial or illusory one, over which to unite, we look at others to project our fears—anything to deflect attention away from ourselves and lives permissibly mislived.

Living Fear Is Fearful Living

"Fearful living" is an oxymoron. In his first book, *Love Is Letting Go of Fear*, California psychiatrist Gerald Jampolsky, now a passionate proponent of conscious living, wrote of the impossibility of the human animal's "living a life, especially loving, when functioning from a place of fear." He pointed to the fact that we cannot love if we are fearful of anything, let alone of each other or our enemies. In fact, we cannot live freely, creatively, and lovingly if we are fearful of life, fearful about our worthiness, or fearful of those who have hurt or attacked us. Moreover, most of us are not aware that it is fear that is at the core of our discomfort, disillusionment, and vigilance in merely performing our daily duties.

Most of us, having been kicked in the heart "ten times or another," have encased our hearts in the psychic equivalent of repressive steel. We have programmed ourselves to misfunction in fear states—that is, in states defined by false expectations that actualize realities. To maintain the consistency of this sane insanity, we then wire ourselves to collect false evidence that appears to be real.

This is how we create realities that are thematically and practically consistent with our encoded expectations and how we calculate possible if dangerous degrees of interconnectedness with others. We either make a judgment about someone prior to meeting him and then gather (self-interpreted) evidence to support our judgment or, even in friendship, become displeased with someone, keep it to ourselves, gather false evidence, and then arbitrarily dismiss that person from our lives.

Perhaps, as is the case with too many people I have treated, there has been so much loss in our lives that loss is easy and rejection a habitual gesture. On the other hand, gain and comfort are foreign states. Either way, it is fearful living doing the gravest of injustices. Indeed, judging to mentally manufacture another person—a distinctly human skill—is to virtually nullify him. A too common form of mental murder, it is among our most primitive abilities.

The Four-Letter Word Stops Action

Fear is the other F word, and it has the opposite effect of the most important, positive F word in the English language: *forgiveness*. Fear violates us and others. It is an emotional thief that can leave us empty and closed to all possibility. In fact, if we wish and yearn from a place of fear, we attract what we fear, consciously or unconsciously, not what we "wish" for with less passion. Even wishing that we were less fearful further encodes the fact that there is something of which we should remain afraid.

"The only thing we have to fear is fear itself," Franklin Delano Roosevelt told the American people in the midst of the 1930s Depression, echoing a truism expressed by commentators from the author of the Old Testament *Proverbs* to the great British general the Duke of Wellington.

Psychologically sound, the assertion suggests that fear has to be acted against in order to be defeated and eliminated. And it has to be challenged repeatedly today, when the unknown is standard. The death knell is the statement "but I've never done it before," meaning that something cannot be done (particularly if that something is right, kind, new, or controversial). We *cannot* live—grow—without day-to-day confrontation with that which makes us insecure or fearful. Nothing to do with creative, fulfilled living is done without passing through either fear based on our personal histories or fear of controversy.

Sadly, the latter appears to defeat us even more frequently than the former. It is no wonder that new ideas, the industrial benchmarks of genius, were and are created and initiated by those exiled in various ways from the comforting stasis of convention.

Approach Fear in a New Way

In today's world, we have to better understand and take a new approach to fear (just as we have to learn a new computer program virtually weekly). Avoidance, which worked quite nicely for years, just doesn't cut it anymore. Neither the business of applying ourselves to a life's work nor the business of relationships can be done in fear. An aspect of conscious living—living that is self-aware and contributive—requires that we actively confront those things that we might, in the past, have left to fester or unwind as they would.

Ironically, this time of having to risk facing our fears has not come during a lull in human life. Rather, it is a time when there is more to fear, generally and specifically, than ever before—more that is new, untried, and intensely consequential. Indeed, it is also a time when confronting our fears is critical for our literal survival. Fear of each other is killing us. Particularly in the western world, our basic human need for closeness and support is a silent scream that suffuses our rushed, multitasked lives and collapsing social structures. The need to trust and to feel secure in something, with some people, and in some places are requisites to our ability to live, to contribute, and to stay sane. As scientists study the increasing occurrence of asthma—the inability to breathe, which is the latest North American epidemic manifestation of empty living—many of us just shake our heads and wipe away another tear. What must we lose before we become sufficiently afraid to find the courage to confront the fears of everyday life?

We have to start with our fear of each other. The most valuable lesson I ever learned came to me years ago from the late Ernest Becker, the anthropologist who wrote *The Denial of Death*. When I was a very young student, he took me aside and explained the suffusing, deleterious pandemic of human fear. He told me to remember, whenever I was fearful, that every other sane, well-meaning person was and always would be at least as fearful as I. He spoke of his own fear, his seemingly insurmountable shyness, as well as of the fear of other great thinkers and writers present in the academic setting in which we met.

Since that moment, not one day has gone by during which I have not thought of our conversation. That piece of critical wisdom has enabled me to get past my own fears, doing hundreds, perhaps thousands of things I would not have done had I not been so informed. It has also allowed me to better understand and address the fears of others.

Understanding that others are afraid, especially those who have injured us, helps us through the process of forgiveness. Indeed, it makes Principle 2's active forgiveness easier to undertake. Reaching out takes courage, as does seeking to understand and reconnect.

Even more courage and understanding of the killing fields of fear are required when one is personally or professionally rebuked by the most intensely (if unconsciously) afraid among the fearful. We most need courage and dignity not in moments of high drama or in situations that require calling 911 but in moments when mere kindness, attentiveness, or understanding are absent because of our contrived determination to remain in control, in blind and deaf denial of the shared neediness of the human animal. No risk—or virtue—is involved in minding one's own business when someone else is fearfully needy. Neither is there any semblance of grace in our inclination to just walk by something that offends or frightens us.

Daily Heroism, Daily Courage

Courage defeats fear, and heroism is being courageous every day of our lives. Most of our daily hurts and compounded fears are both manageable and defeatable. Indeed, for the most part, our fears are not of serial killers and car accidents but of each other. Our need for acceptance from our peers is sweetly pathetic and can be pitifully incapacitating. Unless we are egoists afflicted with a personality disorder, we feel more than we can bear to feel, primarily in relation to interaction and connectedness with each other.

Compounding our fear, hurt, and ultimate numbness is the fact that some of us—ideally, all of us—must be the ones to start to risk passing through the layer of fear that separates us. We have to generate a wave of relief from mutual distrust. We are smothering in our own stifled cries for closeness, for understanding, and often for mere explanation.

I have more patients suffering from words of ever-lasting loyalty and commitment having turned inexplicably to dead silence or to verbal or physical violence than from any other affliction. Verbal violence cruelly frightens and injures us as human animals, and we use it on each other with impunity, aware of but ignoring the consequences. The damage it does forms the basis for much of our feeling of rejection. It is also frequently the method of choice for eliminating individuals from organizations and associations. And the damage is cumulative. Our self-preserving behavior in the face of fear and rejection increases the number of emotional cripples among us. It also leaves fewer and fewer people who have anything to contribute from the heart—and who have the inclination and strength to do so.

Even if the debate on gun control does not interest us, we should be excited about the possibilities inherent in mind, heart, and mouth control. Unless we are ill, caught up in a moment of anger, or otherwise temporarily emotionally disabled, the risk of courageous connections and mutual mollification is incumbent on us as human beings. We *are* responsible for each other and *must* tend to each other, whether in a grocery lineup, in traffic, at the dinner table, or in our offices and work spaces.

The greatest and most powerful impediment to individual, global, and human progress is fear and mutual exclusion.

Yet this threat also gives us our greatest weapon in the quest for life. Who among us will first dare to put down the sword or to challenge false walls and walk beyond old, shared wounds? Who will have the courage to impose mere sanity on our environments? Many are willing. They are working diligently down the hall or taking long walks contemplating how to bridge the gap between pretending to follow some politically correct protocol and really connecting to, sharing with, and supporting other people. Someone, somewhere has to be sufficiently courageous to speak the unspeakable, and someone else has to be sufficiently courageous to not laugh nervously or sneer with common disdain.

The latter reaction is all the permission that the *really* scary people need to dismiss the ineffable truth. Frankly, fearfully angry, prejudiced, unthinking, and stunted beings, with template conversational guides and access to telephones and word processors scare me as much as would bowling leagues turned terrorist groups. From and around the limited, inner workings of imitative non-minds, fear is spread and fed. Far gone, this genre of human mutation (a huge disappointment to Darwin) defines a fine, proper day as one that includes at least one emotional lynching—with "please" and "thank you" on both sides of the show.

Yet by managing our own fear, our attraction to fear in others, and our related perceptions and behavior, we can make a proper day one of joy, rather than blind, habitual cruelty.

A Place

No place or space exists for us, the human animal, to live and give in fear. Just as the lesser mammals must be kept sanguine in order to reproduce, produce, or become nourishment for humans, we cannot feed our world as tight-necked, fist-clenched incubators of fear.

Many years ago, Sigmund Freud wrote of the global damage perpetrated by human fear. Others continue to write of that daily damage to the human heart. Yet currently, without courageous individual and institutional initiatives, we continue to live in and perpetrate distinctly unsafe places and defensively active Selves.

CASE STUDY

Bill and Mary Confront Their Fear of Life

As a therapist, I have long been fascinated by agoraphobia—the fear of wide open spaces or of leaving one's home (of going out). I am increasingly interested now that statistics show that the average working Canadian chooses, because of anxiety and exhaustion, not to go out in the evening on a work night as often as he did even three years ago. Further, among the same anxious majority more than 70 percent have difficulty getting up in the morning to go to work.

Indeed, the second-fastest growth industry in Canada is the manufacture and sale of security systems, much in demand even in low-crime areas. Evidently, increasing the sense of safety or security that one feels at home has become more important to us as our worlds have become more complex and disturbing. With individual employees saying that they feel unsafe (disturbed, insecure, unsure) at work, *home* has taken on a whole new meaning. For many employed North Americans, it has become more a place to flee to for protective custody than a place to be with family and to re-create.

A case in point was Bill, a 47-year-old man who came to me for counseling, along with his wife, Mary, after the couple found it had become increasingly difficult—eventually, almost impossible—to get up and get to work. Each of their employers had been talking about reorganizing, with some employees working out of their homes, and both spouses had put in to be on the list. But as yet, it hadn't happened.

Their difficulty with going to work had become noticeable about three years earlier. Then it was primarily Bill who waited (and complained) as long as possible before he bit the bullet and headed to his car for the drive to the office. Mary, although also "pained by the process," could still manage to get herself up and dressed, push Bill along, get the kids to school, and then get out the door herself. Even then, however, both of them would check their watches and grit their teeth all day until they could make a break for the comfortable imprisonment of home.

Bill had also developed insomnia. Twice he had acquired physicians' letters verifying that he was too fatigued to work and that he needed a week off. Mary, dealing with her own anxiety, Bill's building anxiety, the problems of raising a preteen and two teenagers, eventually saw the same doctor and acquired the same permission to be absent from what both spouses had started to refer to as the houses of horrors.

By the time the two came for counseling, each had received warnings from their workplace manager. They were neither productive nor reliable, and their comfortable office jobs were on the line. They had also started to use over-the-counter sleep- and wakeup-aids by the carton. And they were arriving at their offices later and leaving earlier as the weeks went by.

Bill and Mary are not uncommon. First, they were fearful of change, as are most mammals. As a result, fundamental changes at their workplaces unnerved them to the point of physical discomfort. Second, both felt insufficiently valuable to their firms to be left in their current position. Their shared sense of worthlessness had them waiting for termination (perceived as virtual death). Third, as is sadly the case with many people, neither trusted anyone other than the other (and that not always) and one or two members of their families. So if anything happened around them at work, they suspected it had something to do with them personally, but no one was telling them. Yet because of their lack of trust and fear of others, neither ever asked what was happening or would happen at the office. They didn't dare show any lack of knowledge, which they thought might appear to be stupidity. As a result, the question marks continued to add up until they created a psychic mountain in each of their hearts and minds. They then shared their mountains with each other, highlighting and speculating about a nonreality of their own almost paranoiac construction.

Obviously, this situation could not go on without affecting their family. The children were suffering from the siege mentality in the house, and Sunday nights had become scene nights with inevitable fights, sometimes physical ones, as everyone tensed up for the next week of war. Bill and Mary had polluted their relationship, their family, and their home with fear.

To a layperson, that fear might appear to be a fear of nothing. It was, however, very real to them and extremely debilitating. They had lived nearly to middle age without having to face issues related to their value, their competency, their beliefs about the nature of life itself, or their not-so-inordinate fear of others. Then the upheaval in today's workplaces brought all their semi-latent fears to the surface and activated behavior that had been, for the most part, in check. They preferred to imprison themselves in a dark cave of apparent safety than to face newness or a shift in their reality.

What it all came down to was a basic fear of and insecurity about various aspects of themselves. Moreover, it not only paralyzed them and drove them to urgent, intense counseling; it also modeled for their children a picture of the world that could be disastrous. At least one of their children, a preteen boy, caught the fear bug, believing that if mom and dad were so afraid of the world out there, there must be something monstrous to protect oneself against. He happened to have a fascination with guns. Well into his parents' therapy, he joined them in a discussion about his fears and his feelings of defensiveness. (Living in what is, for all intents and purposes, a non-firearms culture, the young man and others were at less risk than if he had resided elsewhere.)

Bill and Mary had to work on their basic, individual issues, assist each other by not spiraling into fear states together, and literally practice going to work fearlessly. After two years, they are better but, along with a majority of the silently frightened, still expend too much energy merely getting to a place to earn income.

Fear in this form (and others) is epidemic and renders people like Bill and Mary pathetic and emotionally (sometimes literally) impoverished.

EXERCISE

Today and everyday, observe the fearfulness of others. Also, take notice of what frightens you and act, *not in retaliation but in understanding*. Know that courage is not the absence of fear but the adult ability to go on in spite of fear.

Further, note the cumulative inner effects of random acts of courageous contribution—the only way to an ultimate win-win endeavor or relationship. If you are afraid of or resistant to someone, ascertain why, from the inside out. If someone rebukes your earnest attempt at courageous connecting or reconnecting, leave that individual in his place of sad imprisonment, wish him well, and move on, beyond the toxicity, to honest, creative personhood.

Last, work to create spaces and places of peaceful tranquility for yourself and others.

Principle 4

Observation and Judgment

Look for the depth of goodness and strengths (as well as the vulnerability) in others, rather than judging others for their fallibility.

Some people believe that we were all born and remain divinely perfect. Others, in both their attitudes and their behaviors, make it eminently clear that they perceive much of the human race as curs.

Aaron Holtzman, a Soviet immigrant recently arrived in the United States

Each time I look into the eyes of an animal, I see the sweet, reflected vulnerability of all the animals I have ever loved and lost. I can be brought to my knees in public places, kissing and hugging a pet with a tolerant owner who shares my infinite, unconditional love for animals. Animals, tamed or untamed, are open to love. Many of us have had similarly loving experiences with children under age five or six, before they have been responsibly, repressively inculcated with the notion that all strangers are dangerous. My eyes meet theirs, a connection is made for connection's sake, and a rapport is created, usually based on shared smiles, silliness, and a fascination with the awesomely mundane.

I *try* to love adult humans this way. In most adults, I am able to see the infant, a once-helpless life form held in the arms of an adoring mother. Street people in particular move me this way. So do people from other cultures, visible minorities, and even those who hold opinions or perform actions that I find difficult to accept *if* I consciously revisualize them as individuals with their own beginnings and unknown journeys. Alternatively, when I am potentially irritated by someone, I try to practice patience by imagining that they are a century old and that I can acquire great wisdom from them. Each of these strategies is useful during an age when we are all time-challenged, inveterately impatient, and defensively quick to judge.

Yet it is difficult to remain neutrally accepting of those we encounter in the day-to-day tizzies that frequently define millennial life. Although I take risks (for example, by smiling at and speaking to strangers when there is no reason to—culturally, an almost indictable offense), I cannot give to other, closed-off adults as consistently as I give to their children or their pets, even if the latter are goldfish. On bad days, the possibility of a complete lack of response or of a squint-eyed look of fearful curiosity discourages me from trying to relate. And sometimes I join the majority of North Americans who just walk on by, choosing not to look at all— in lineups, on airlines, even with long-time car pool associates. It seems not worth the effort. We all have an enormous will to love, but we leave it in retraction until we have several guarantees that our love will be accepted, not rejected and thrown back at our hearts.

As adult human animals, whose innate fear of each other is a scientific fact, we should look more often into each other's eyes and correctly perceive the depth of vulnerability, basic goodness, and need with which we all live. For the most part, we avoid eyes and miss the shift, the positive or at least significant movement in our hearts that comes with the possibility of connecting at the windows of souls.

Universal Vulnerability

Virtually everyone feels vulnerable in the face of myriad changes in our lifestyle, including, among uncountable other things, changes in our workplaces and in the nature of our work. As vulnerable beings, we are too often in defensive mode, learning and adjusting on the spot, nervously awaiting the next personal disruption.

Further, most organizations today either are temporarily without leadership (something we still look to for answers and solutions to the insoluble) or are under the aegis of the "new leadership" that requires that we think, say, do, decide, and risk much more in the way of personal responsibility. Studies show that without prior learning and with virtually no practice in that approach, we tend to hunker down, rather than face the fire.

Moreover, we tend to stay in defensive, intensive, and eventually alienating postures in all aspects of our lives. As workers, parents, taxpayers, budgeters, shoppers, cleaners, drivers, and so on, we get through the average day in high gear (or, to use the medical term, with an eroding adrenaline rush). This state is compounded by the pace at which we have to respond to edicts from colleagues and memoranda and from a constant flow of faxes, e-mails, and voice mail messages. In fairness to those who can still conceive of closeness, there is little time to stop and check out the unique and complex humanity of those who blur by us in a day or week. Just when we need connections more than ever, we seem to have no time for valid connections of a mutually accepting and supportive kind.

Further, in our frenzied, defensive mental and metabolic rush, when we do brush past each other, we are likely to infer a negative rather than a positive. This perception is a result of sheer reflex. High-gear, high-speed, defensive living, which is unnatural to the human animal, induces a state of mammalian reactivity. When overstimulated, we are emotionally and physically vigilant, incapable of a reasoned and rational assessment of others.

This situation is hardly an asset for team-building, and it has to be considered and addressed by human resource specialists (among others). We are not responding to or addressing each other or our life- or work-tasks the way we did as recently as three to five years ago. We are considerably, reflexively more critical of others (and, naturally, ourselves) and much less prepared to trust others or to work in synchronicity with them.

Scheduled Blindness

In the midst of our rushed lives and often overwhelming obligations, we miss and dismiss opportunities for revealing connections, partially because we are living on the defensive. We speed through our days in defense against time and too often, as discussed under other principles, in defensive postures regarding each other and ourselves. Thus, we are hard pressed to acknowledge and be aware of our *own* vulnerability and basic goodness, let alone those of others. Moreover, given a lifestyle in which we function in various kinds and degrees of self-defense (from the complex psychological to the immunological), we are, even as good, noncombative people, infinitely more likely to perceive the bad in another person than we are to feel-find the good. The sheer velocity with which we compete with time leaves virtually no time for life-enriching, even lifesaving connections unless we opt for sanity and make time.

We need to slow down and to touch down with each other—even, with tacit or overt permission, to appropriately touch each other in recognition of our common need for acceptance. Our surfaces reveal little if anything about who we are. Thus, we ensure (or attempt to ensure) our protection. Our eyes, however, tell much about our bravery, our persistent struggles, our shared losses and fears. What and who we are is evident in our eyes, and if we really look, we rarely find evidence of true nastiness or deliberate malevolence in the eyes of others or of ourselves. Indeed, most of us avoid fully looking at ourselves in a mirror. We avoid our own eyes because we do not want to see what it is that we mask all day, each day, as we play our roles in the world. We know what we would see, and it would, if really examined, diminish our ability to maintain our homogenizing demeanor. Similarly, if we were to look at others, we would see the strain of self-concealment, the essence of what lies behind the pact we have made with each other to maintain distance and a blind, unfeeling efficiency.

Reactive Protection

Rapid, unpredictable change exacerbates our personal fears. Insecurities that we thought had disappeared reemerge and become more intense. And we become harder, apparently even more uncaring and intolerant as we unconsciously arm ourselves for an undefined battle. Our own eyes, if someone were to look, show hurt, fear, and fatigue, as do the avoided eyes of people we deem either ignorable or offensive. We are actually mirroring each other in a state of systemic and irrationally mortal fear.

Sudden change, which is sudden loss and confusion, make us skittish animals with enormous brains, unconsciously clutching our sense of existence. On an unconscious level, studies have shown, we literally fear for our lives. For thousands of years, our neurophysiology was appropriately programmed to consciously and unconsciously perceive danger in and react to more primitive versions of the lifestyle cataclysms many of us are now experiencing in our daily lives.

Yet we are now expected to function, even better than last year, with creativity and connectedness. This paradigm paradox, wherein new, unleashed brain power and creativity are required at a time when most brains are on emergency pause—less agile, open, or capable than ever—is at the center of our renewed vulnerability and problematic reactivity. Incredulous and unprepared for what has befallen us (actually a positive opportunity in the long run), we just do our best in fearful anticipation of messing up or of being ousted from environments that have ever-changing requisites for acceptability.

We were not educated for and did not ask for a mandate for change and growth. We thought we had learned the earlier lessons well and had, therefore, earned our right to secure living. We now avoid eyes more than ever (not ever having been overly friendly beasts) in a pervasive state of humiliation—and of muted anger and fear. We hide, rather than reside, alongside each other, awaiting the next seemingly impossible challenge or crisis. And given this shared mind-body posture, with no one looking beyond the surface of performance and mere motion, we convincingly cross-convey failure, blame, and competitive contempt—in reality, versions and degrees of terror-hardened tears.

Broken Bonds: A Defence

In my work, both one-on-one and in groups, I observe firsthand today's human defense mechanisms at work. Too frequently, I am asked to provide a team-building exercise for bright but frightened individuals who are well past the point of being able to accept high school metaphors or to return to the models of another albeit recent era.

The commendable concept of building teams was based on mutual recognition and organization of strengths. It was also contingent upon willingness, goodwill, trust, and a belief in a shared, mutually beneficial purpose. Bona fide teams supported risk-taking in clearer climates.

Much of the team-building asked of employees and managers in today's organizations is impossible under current psychological, operational, and "ideational" conditions. This is not to say that the concept (or reality) of working teams is dead. It is to say, however, that before such units can exist anew, much work must be done to bridge the fear-induced, blinding gaps between and among participants.

Teams require a synergistic intimacy. It is no coincidence that they are still critical to the functioning of units of police, paramedics, surgeons, and others who work in high-risk, high-consequence emergency operations. Within these teams, the purpose is shared and clear, the skills required are set, and on-the-spot decision-making is necessarily decentralized. The members have no choice but to trust each other in meeting ever-changing challenges with instant innovation and decisive risk-taking. They understand the urgency of success and automatically share the ramifications of triumph and failure. By necessity, interactions and responses are judgment-free, and resourceful interpersonal communication just happens. The objective is to provide service to the "client," the unit, and to each invaluable member. There is no time for the luxury of false judgment, opting out, or apathy. The quality of service is distinctively measurable in terms of life and death.

Mismanaged Diversity

Unfortunately, too many organizations do have time for false protocols and judgments with respect to acceptable communication. The politically correct, delicately artificial interaction and communication in most growing and adjusting corporations condone both cautious, habitual superficiality and fear-induced, systemic blindness. This syndrome is antithetical to the critical mandate of the new leadership; floundering traditional structures still depend on inactive listening and the dismissal of the anomalous.

Potential bonds and productive connections among employees and managers are further impeded by an ill-thought-out quick fix for the sensitivity and depth of knowledge and understanding required to really manage diversity. An approach universally accepted in North America has, seemingly without causing much concern, made the issue of difference easier to ignore. Interestingly, at the heart of what are outdated and dangerously unnatural policies of "speak no evil, hear no evil, imply no evil, but report *all and any* semblance of evil" is a built-in prejudice toward intimacy and trust. These policies demand that virtually nothing of any questionability be said to or about anyone, especially men and women or members of identifiable racial groups or ethnic minorities. Any attempt at even intelligent humor, the greatest unifier of statesmen and street gangs alike, is perceived as tantamount to bringing an Uzi to work!

These policies allow us to be politely silent and literally ignoring of our colleagues of distinction. Thus, for yet another systemic reason, we remain disconnected from and unaware of the strengths, weaknesses, and talents of valuable human resources. More important, we just preclude the protected, leaving talented groups of employees and neighbors isolated and out—more out than we feel.

Now, with affirmative action having faded into the static created by louder and more urgent issues related to millennial adaption, we will presumably have less to be politically preclusive about and fewer souls to politely, correctly ignore. Time will tell a more harrowing story, I am afraid, because of our apparent inability to deal in anything other than the tidy fantasy of nonwhite and white (mostly white).

I have often run into this issue of preclusive distinction in my work as a speaker. For example, with carefully, strategically applied humor, I deliberately highlight the differences between men and women as they relate to each other in work and other partnerships. Indeed, I use the latest studies from the top business schools in North America, as well as mental health studies, to address the ways in which we can and must recognize and utilize, instead of merely avoid, the differences between and among us. But I am always aware of some hypersensitivity related to talking out loud about, for example, task-related gender differences. Indeed, I have been booked by female agents who simply assume that the issue will not be discussed even if it is an integral part of a contractual agreement.

Many people are still permittedly resistant to mutual recognition of visible minorities and are shocked to hear the fact actually addressed aloud. It is a challenge to admit that most of us have, in accordance with traditional organizational policy, found convenient ways to further dismiss and quietly discredit each other. The same is true for policies established to condemn racism. Women, ethnic minorities, and people of color are further isolated by virtue of policies that inadvertently but effectively separate us, rather than unite us. In fact, both men and women, as well as members of myriad minorities, suffer from such policies as much or more than they would if no policies existed. No one says anything spontaneous to anyone else for fear of a misunderstanding or miscommunication, even potential litigation.

Overall, we are following antiquated rules that preclude attunement and mutual consideration, not to mention communication and synergistic creativity. Ironically, such policies ensure that the characteristics, needs, and strengths we share remain unacknowledged and inaccessible. In a manner that is neither humanly sane nor organizationally intelligent, weaknesses and strengths go unrecognized because of our blunt determination to delicately position difference, the inherently unpositionable. In the name of specious, sweep-it-under-the-carpet protocol, too many of us in too many workplaces are missing opportunities to create a shared sense of purpose, to unify and integrate our strengths and talents to meet both general and specific objectives related to human innovation and growth.

Hide and Seek

Since we were children, we have heard that we should look for the best in others. In fact, this admonishment sits deep in our subconscious as something else that we should and would be doing consistently were we good kid-adults. Needless to say, this is the worst way we can think about issues of connection and goodwill with others, regardless of the context. We need, consciously and in the present, to be more aware of the complexity of other people. When we see, without reason or provocation, monstrous images in others, those images are mirrors of our own self-doubts and fears. And when we are fearful and insecure in our environment, we unconsciously deem almost everyone who comes into our space to be contributing to our personal instability. Consequently, we are likely to look no further toward understanding than the short-sighted strictures our insecurity and fear allow.

We are the only living creatures who can "cross-context" our fear—that is, who, when afraid, can find something negative or fearful in virtually everything and everyone else. Moreover, we do not have to be psychologically abnormal to act this way; it is merely if problematically human. We rescind our goodwill and attentiveness when we feel insecure and experience our lives as chaotic. The lifestyle and work-style changes we are facing are, therefore, playing havoc with our otherwise relatively sane psyches.

Compounding our blind, indirectly judgmental reactivity is the other basic need peculiar to the human animal: the need for stability and clarity of purpose. We have needed this since we lived in primitive villages, and when we have not had it, we have more often than not created conflict—something to be against—as a focus of purposeful activity. In recent days, we have all seen this phenomenon in places where at least some of us felt we engaged in meaningful labor. In fear for ourselves and without an evident sense of purpose, we roam in packs of one, pondering our fate and suspecting the worst of situations and of others. The validity of insecurity-inducing chaos aside, it is us we are confronting and each other we are doubting in the absence of a reason to trust and accept.

In brief, this period of human history is a difficult time for a post-modern, western human being to have to look to other members of the species for supportive kindness and strength. It was easier to help each other, even to be down-home honest with each other, when that was just the nice thing to do if we had time or were in the mood. Now, seeking out the good in others is a mutually beneficial necessity. If we work and live in places where things have come apart (and new leadership has not yet helped us come together), *we* have to find or create purpose in our interactions. The end crisis will come when we have lost both purpose and people. The current statistics on the mental health of the average organizational employee are a scary portent.

A middle manager recently told me, "Even if Bambi were to approach me, I'd wanna punch her! I'd attack before I got it! I don't trust anybody!" For the majority of the working population of North America, neither Bambi nor Thumper would be the first choice of defining names for their closest colleagues. Without special consideration, we can't see the sweetness or the nonaggressive fear and confusion in the fundamentally innocent eyes of other lost and frightened souls. Without realizing the self-destruction wrought by separation and judgment, we have not had a good enough reason to look.

Old Postures That Die Hard

Indeed, our current lifestyle and our exacerbated personal insecurities have made us blind and presumptive when it comes to accepting and connecting with others. At work, despite the latest corporate or organizational posture, we still perceive our colleagues as competitors of whom we should remain afraid and around whom we should remain vigilant. As a result, we increasingly isolate ourselves, hoarding our knowledge and skills, hoping to be among the winners rather than the losers.

No one argues the basic logic of establishing win-win situations, but very few try to apply the concept. Increasingly, when I speak with groups of people undergoing massive changes in their work and personal lives, they admit to feeling that they *cannot* risk sharing their experience or knowledge with coworkers. More often than not both insecure and on the defensive, they think, as an employee in a seminar said recently, "I ain't look'n out for his ass, I'm look'n out for mine! I'll speak to the guy, but he ain't getting my help! Why should he? No one's helping me!" The depth of this angry logic is typical. To frightened, hurt, and demoralized human beings, it seems absurd that they should be expected to cooperate and work synergistically with the competition, essentially the enemy. Old paradigms die hard—especially under pressure.

Our resistance to sharing and our inclination to judge and reject are not only premillennial or millennial reactions (although both are intensified by rapid transition and insecurity). In our competitive, Calvinistic, quasi-individualistic (yet obedient and dependent) culture, most people are inclined, from very early on, to reject others rather than accept them, to keep them at bay rather than consciously or unconsciously induce closeness. Perversely, we, as an insecure culture, are more interested in the bad than the good in others. Someone else's failure or fall from grace is both fascinating and comforting. Somehow, we are better if someone else is worse. We are okay if it is someone else who gets into trouble, faces a crisis, or loses her job.

Furthermore, most of us can remember from childhood the emphasis on strength and self-reliance over any display of weakness. In fact, we were taught to feel contempt for fallibility and frailty in others as well as in ourselves. As a result, when we feel increasingly fallible (lost and inadequate) and weak (ineffective), we are increasingly hard on ourselves, and we apply the same impossibly cruel standards to others. Ten years ago we might have allowed some latitude for vindication, but in our current state of tight-fisted isolation, we don't or can't give an inch. As children, we sat in neatly separated rows of politely presumptuous little faces, and we learned our narrow lessons well, assuming a life-long warranty based on mere obedience. We were never taught the relationship between our brains, our hearts, and our behaviors. We were processed to be exactly where we are now. But now is another world suddenly, systematically requiring significantly more of our humanity, something most of us have left unexplored, let alone fully applied. We have rarely been consciously exposed to the magic and true meaning and effect of being human.

Win-Win Behavior

Now we *have* to take the time, as we go about our insanely busy lives, to risk both accepting and being accepted by others. If only because we are too tired and too beaten by our reactivity to expend energy on the illusory relief that comes with anger and blame, we have to back off from our own inclination toward self-protective attack. As isolated and defensive as we already are, we are approaching each day of our shortening lives as if we were engaged in polite, usually bloodless warfare.

As I repeat ad nauseam in my public teaching, win-win strategies, cooperation, sharing knowledge, "connecting and communicating," and so on are not just new visionary and operational mandates dictated by corporations in order to increase productivity (even though the application of these inordinate concepts is critical to achieving that goal). Fortunately for us, they are also human behavioral lifesavers, and we should celebrate the mandate. It is about time that certain behaviors are deemed more appropriate and more valuable than others. Perhaps still long in the coming, mutual acceptance and kindness may become dicta in our organizations, not just the buzz words of the month. If sensitive, supportive, and empathetic behaviors were mandated, we would have a reason—indeed, we would be forced—to undo our years of training in exclusionary competition and the reflexive dismissal of other human minds and hearts. As a bonus, there would also be a tangible incentive to look more deeply into each other and to connect at the level of mirrored commonality.

Mirroring, Magic, and Acceptance

In my life's work with the human heart, I am sometimes now able to see in the eyes of a stranger, the reflections of the eyes of the many individuals I have come to love and to comprehend. Although I work at this exercise within a culture whose citizens have a tacit agreement to neither look at nor touch each other, the results of my attempts have been enriching—invariably for me and sometimes for the stranger with whom I connect. Blissfully though painfully, I am increasingly able to see in other eyes pain and (less often) joy reflecting my own. Regardless of the person, the place, or the circumstances, virtually any individual can evoke in me—in anyone—compassion and comfort as well as a natural will toward kindness.

I am not referring only to the nonthreatening elderly, the disabled, and playful, jump-suited toddlers. They are *easy* for us to love, to be generous with, and to leave unjudged. I am referring to prison inmates, panhandlers, young delinquents who display sociopathic cruelty, and people whose color and cultural habits are completely foreign, even discomfiting. The seemingly magical but merely common connectedness that occurs when one really looks at another person and acknowledges her unique grace and heroism is among the most pleasant and sacred of human experiences. Or, it can and should be.

We all, of course, need the same latitude for acceptance. If statistics mean anything, the large majority of those who read this book need to be given a chance to just be without being evaluated or judged, and also to be affirmed. There are times when someone catches my eye as I wander through my daily duties, deep in thought or saddened with concern, and I find myself close to tears after such a connection. It is touching to be noticed, neutrally or positively, for just being.

We live lives in which we are and feel judged, in one way or another, much more often than we are given and can take the gift of acceptance. The way we look, what we do, how we live, whom we live with, whether we work and what we work at leave us open to the defensive hypercriticism of others in a social framework that, ironically, otherwise breeds and encourages indifference and noninvolvement. As a result, we are rarely relaxed with our own species. As if we were and always will be the new kid in school, having to prove ourselves but never quite cutting it with the "in" crowd, we too often overperform and undercreate from a place of presumed inadequacy and insecurity.

We have to favor the innate goodness in each other and seek to understand our shared fallibilities. They are each aspects of our workable human complexity. Only when we look at each other in this open way can we start putting into practice (rather than obediently chanting) the concepts of cooperation, mutual support, even consistently sound customer service. Otherwise, in this bizarre, revolutionary period, we will further evolve into unknowing members of a team with the too-common purpose of senseless loss.

CASE STUDY

Paralyzed Employees Get Lost in Reflexive Judgment and Mistrust

A large organization in which I have done some work has a division in which I am sure that someone is going to get hurt. Already, more than one-third of the employees, including managers, have left on either sick leave or leave without pay. The level of stress-related illness is inordinately high, and tempers are raging at a level befitting gang warfare.

By declaration, this workplace is a team environment. However, very few of the approximately 20 staff members show up for meetings, no one wants to take on any tasks, and only one or two people do any work at all. Fringe groups meet to discuss their disgust with the division and its nonmanagement, and senior managers fret to find new ways to justify their division's lack of productivity. All in all, more effort goes into managing simmering conflict than into doing business. No one trusts anyone else enough to share a plan of action, and it would be easier to form a team among opponents in Bosnia Herzegovina.

In short, this is a perfect example of a work environment poisoned by judgment and distrust. Everyone seems to have decided, prima facie, that everyone else is dishonest in some way. Management has been patently irresponsible in not both bringing the staff together and cracking the whip with respect to productivity and performance. The employees are running the show—and there is no show at all. Nine-tenths of increasing morale and productivity is instilling trust and imposing a sense of purpose. Without these key components, humans forced together to do nothing make an activity out of mutual attack, gossip, and internecine cruelty. The only action is massaging the vicious judgment of the day. At the time of this writing, one employee has just attempted suicide—most probably just to get out.

What needs to happen here is a forced meeting of minds (if not hearts). Management has been counseled to show leadership by addressing the internecine warfare and by demanding mutually supportive and productive behavior. It would do well to ask the employees for input on how best to pursue both goals.

EXERCISE

Try to see beyond the exterior of each person you see today, including your spouse or children. Look at your colleagues, managers, employees, and neighbors as if you were seeing them for the first time and had heard only wonderfully positive things about them. Go even further. Pretend that you have heard that they have spoken extremely highly of you, mentioning to others your strengths, talents, and kindness. By so doing, transform, at least momentarily, fearful or defensively negative assumptions and expectations into enthusiastic acceptance and anticipation.

Also, be aware of what happens in your inner world as you make the approach to communicate. Your underlying perspective will shift. You will feel good about the person you approach, and before you utter a word, she will sense this. She will pick up on and act on her side of a tacit mammalian contract regarding acceptance and mutual respect—one that more often than not has nothing to do with our facile use of words.

Principle 5

Connection versus
Dismissal

Try to perceive the poor behavior of others as a call for help, an indication of fear or confusion, rather than as an attack or assault.

As infants we cried and were held or fed. As adolescents we rebelled and
were passively alienated by the uncomprehending and incomprehensible re-
activity of our parents. As adults, we can do neither, but much more that is
destructive. We have power—and when lost or hurt, we use it against each
other with cruel impunity.

Bruno Bettelheim

I spend much time in airports, amazing stopover environments. Although
the same kinds of behaviors turn up in grocery stores, department
stores, and other public places where adults bring their children, somehow
airports always up the ante. Particularly frequent are the cries and squirm-
ings of tired, bedraggled infants and toddlers. When these little ones are
hurt, tired, or just fed up with participating in the lives of adults, they
scream, fall to the floor and refuse to get up, or act out in some other
unselfconscious manner. We adults are touched, amused, or mildly irritated
by such normal childish protest. Many of us are moved by the wails of frustration and exhaustion, perfectly comfortable with a small child's open and
clear expression of needs, and we exchange knowing smiles. Some ob-
servers step in to lend a hand or a hug. The worst that happens is that
someone who has had a rough day retreats to a quieter spot, one where
companions are muted by the protocol of adult repression.

Adults do not cry out, at least not in public and rarely in private. We have become so good as big children that we do not dare express ourselves the way we did as smaller children, when we had full lives and much less to lose. In a powerful and heart-bending way, society has agreed that unpleasant self-expression is at least a misdemeanor, and depending on the context, degree, and form, it may be a major felony.

In Principle 4, I proposed learning to look for the good in others. Here I suggest the flip side of that principle: breaking our habitual, judgmental reactions to unpleasant, unusual, or poor behavior in others and, to a responsible extent, in ourselves. In other words, I ask that we do not just seek out what is positive about other people but that we also try to look beyond what might be perceived as a lack of consideration or an attack. We can do this by attempting to see others from an objective viewpoint, one separate from our own insecurities and agendas. Most of the time, we will find that we are able to feel compassion, rather than defensiveness and ill will.

Being Deaf in the Depths

A colleague and I recently discussed the difference in the freedom of expression "permitted" adults and young children. He had been up all night dealing with his 20-month-old's machinations, and by the time he had to go to work, he himself was on the verge of screaming. Instead, of course, he just dressed for his work role and moved through his duties as a physician to continue to provide a home for his family. He coped, as he says he does most days, with muted anxiety, pent-up frustration, and debilitating fatigue. Had a trusted colleague not asked him about his feelings, he would not have said a word. He was accustomed to sitting on his emotions and dutifully performing to rule because that is what our culture demands adults do. Our lives are increasingly bereft of emotional choices.

We do, however, have our moments. Barring any other way to express the impermissible, our feelings come out in curtness, impatience, or sarcasm. That most of us still wonder what *we* did or said when someone in our sphere seems angry or upset does neither the expresser nor the ostensible victim any good. Moreover, the reflexive assumption is a false one, an imaginary experience with highly toxic consequences that are unnecessary more often than not. Such an assumption simply gives the expresser more anger, more confusion, and more emotion to repress.

We need to allow each other the odd moment of expressed adult displeasure. One reason is the public's comfort, even safety. The acceptable diffusion of grief and anger can keep those of us who are particularly pressured by inner demons from exploding and expressing frustration with an arsenal of ammunition much more damaging and final than words or gestures. (And in the latter case, any victim will do, the focus or reason for the anger having been long lost in the protocol of suppression.)

A second reason is a fundamental concern for others and ourselves. Adulthood has, by virtue of our upbringing, brought with it tacit rules of conduct and tolerance. With limited allowances for youth, certain disabilities, and episodic reactions to personal tragedy, our culture decrees that unpleasant or negative emotions are to be left unexpressed except under the most extreme circumstances. Feelings that are communicated cause discomfort, and some form of obloquy often follows. So why tip the emotional boat in which we all travel?

Anger is the prime example. It is virtually unacceptable among most associations of adults. Expressed by a man, it disturbs and frightens other men as well as women. Expressed by a woman, it is tantamount to an indictable offense. Already in a fear state (or poised for a new or exacerbated one), we are, more often than not, incompetent when faced with open anger. Many of us either leave the scene or just close down, permanently dismissing the perpetrator from our inner circle because of our discomfort and displeasure.

Unfortunately, these scenarios of mismanaging emotions are often played out in workplaces. People who live unconsciously—that is, driven by their subconscious, rather than led by a managed consciousness—are ill-equipped to intelligently accept and express their own emotions or to understand the expressions of others. Yet humans without periodic expressions of intense emotion are beings without the passion critical to high performance, innovation, and satisfaction. They are also individuals who are heartlessly working to rule.

The reflexive retreat from intensely expressed emotions is, ironically, shared by the expresser and the receiver or observer. *Both* are usually loyal to the rigid, black and white dictates governing adult behavior. As a result, most of us expect our world to end when we indulge in intense expression. Having loosened our emotional cork even to a moderate degree, we are pretty sure we will need to make emergency reparations.

Moreover and more significant, we prepare ourselves for the fear-based conflict that usually ensues after an intense or unpleasant burst of emotion. In that we have tacitly agreed, since the lessons of childhood, that an absence of niceties can mean all-out war, the expressive human animal immediately begins to emotionally sandbag. On the defensive, we anticipate a degree of shunning and other forms of admonishment.

We do not like it when someone expresses what we fear and might express ourselves. And unconsciously, we agree to maintain the flow, to leave undisturbed the bland, unchallenging stream of things. The implicit understanding is that we leave much unsaid, and if someone breaks the contract, surface allegiances evaporate, and we scramble in a mass retreat, both to protect ourselves and to furtively condemn. Lost animals, we are misguidedly determined to sustain our walls, petrified of our own common wails.

Crime and Punishment

The punishment is, therefore, swift for those who express themselves beyond the pleasantries of acceptable parlance. Regardless of how steadfast someone may seem in his expression of displeasure, he *expects* the boom to fall. Indeed, when a friend or colleague announces that he has just "lost it" in a meeting, we crowd around him with whispering intrigue and then dissociate quickly as if we too expect a bomb to go off in our midst. As expressive beings who do not express, we expect the end of life as we know it when we or someone else inordinately emotes, rationally or irrationally.

In fact, we are so well-trained in both receiving and dishing out reactive, rejecting measures in the face of the unacceptable that we have difficulty discerning benign responses. Indeed, if one of us breaks the punitive pattern and seeks to *understand* the expression of anger or other nonlethal unpleasantness, the expressor may well be dumbfounded, even potentially threatened by the attempt to hear beyond the outburst.

In a culture of separation, competition, and hidden jealousies, the rule is, don't talk, fight! Responding intelligently and patiently to an expression of displeasure seems to be within the purview of only psychotherapists and pastors. Yet it takes no leap of intelligence to realize that adults, like children, act out when they need something but do not dare ask. Like children, we need, and become frightened and angry. Unlike children, we are so fearful of our own potential for destructive anger that we are resolutely unforgiving of ourselves and others who express their feelings. The mere scent of displeasure or incipient conflict triggers defensive reactivity. Consequently, instead of hearing the cry for help, the frustration, confusion, and fear behind the words of another, we perceive and respond to the expression as if it were a personal attack. And that is the genesis of unhealthy, unnecessary interpersonal conflict.

Increasingly, therefore, our world has little room for creative conflict or controversy. But here is a paradox. A fundamental requirement of the new workplace, *creative* conflict is the only way to discover and to implement new ideas. Passive, consonant thinking is both passé and purposeless. Nothing much gets done if the basic mandate is to maintain calm and calming seas. Environments defined by controlled ideas, monotonal expressiveness, and a polite absence of intense disagreement do not produce or survive. The static that is a natural byproduct of sharing new ideas and the elements of endeavors is healthy and usually productive. Unfortunately, workplace studies show that most people prefer to work alone so as to avoid the discomforting fizz that results from the mere meeting of minds.

Parenting the Program

As adults who have been trained to be fearful and to avoid conflict, we do a disservice to the often appropriate machinations of those who want to authentically contribute to work and other endeavors. Unfortunately, many of us deal similarly with our children. Uncomfortable with inordinancy ourselves, we tend to allow little latitude for self-expression. Although we presumably want preadolescents and adolescents to grow into thoughtful, responsible, interesting, and interested adults, we teach them early on to censor their flexing certitude and curiosity. We warn them and teach them by example to keep their mouths shut whenever there is any sign of consequential dissonance. Thus, we pass on the cultural imperative to avoid rocking emotional boats.

Many of us apply this genre of safe living much more intensely than we risk the antithetical posture of conscious living—that is, emotive but responsible, respectful, and managed self-expression. Were we able to model the ways and means of expression *including* displeasure, we would succeed more often as parents and be less frequently horrified by the desperate acting out of an otherwise manageable child.

Often, when we are faced with other people's children, even long after they pass toddler age, we know that when they are mad, they are sad. If we are secure ourselves, we deal with them accordingly, listening rather than lambasting. Were we able to do this more consistently with our own children, we would be more likely to raise viable, flexible, and employable adults, beings confident that their ideas can and should be expressed. Instead of fearing provocation or the inducement of conflict and the punitive exile that comes with it, youngsters can and should know that conflict is normal, that their feelings and opinions have value, and that they have a say in the nature and quality of their environment and relationships. If we risked acting on that understanding, we could contribute to limiting the negative conflict that grows out of the suppression of positive conflict.

Yet knowing the extreme rejection and exile suffered by nonconformists, we tend, with protective intensity, to teach the old way well. Further, we reinforce the lesson by reacting to our own children in a way that is counterproductive to teaching responsible self-expression. As soon as they can articulate feelings and opinions that are contrary to our own, especially those that come close to our historic sore spots, we teach them the lesson of negative conflict: that ideas unshared by or unpleasant to the listener are to be left unexpressed. An opinion not held by others is still, even in an age of brainstorming and so-called democratic input, initially an inducement to covert conflict and ultimately to attack.

A child who has been fortunate enough to be guided through this insanity early on generally finds her way through the psychological landmines. Moreover, she is significantly less inclined than many to lash out at inordinate expression herself, and she tends to ask for new ideas, opinions, and solutions. Having had some latitude for selfhood and self-expression in childhood, she is able, as an adult, to recognize its importance to life and to creating with others; she is also aware of the consequences of its absence.

Adults who value real individual freedom of expression sense that in environments of all kinds, when human beings stop expressing, asking for, and sharing new knowledge and ideas, conflict becomes the filler. One way or another, our behavior and our ideas—or, in contrast, our mental-emotional stasis—affect each other. When we join the tacit agreement to say and give nothing to our ostensibly shared endeavors, we are holding each other in unstated but evident contempt. If we say aloud what needs to be said and done, we may be perceived as storming the walls of a strong social fortress. An expresser of newness or even of a useful unpleasantness can become a target of fear-based hostility. But we can learn and we can teach our children that when we dare to express ourselves regardless of consequences, we then have to learn quiet, anticipatory dignity—another posture inherent in and defining of the challenge of active personhood. We are right to express; we are wrong to attack. Knowing the difference, even if others do not, is all that should count in both responsible living and new and improved environments.

Shutting Down and Shutting Out

One of the reasons we human beings are so intransigently reactive to and unforgiving of whatever offends, frightens, or insults us is our general fear of each other. As discussed in Principle 3, fear is the greatest obstacle to acceptance and active insight and also to wanting and seeking to understand. Given that we are almost all afraid, neither the offender nor the victim or observer of inordinate expression is willing to risk further investigation in an emotionally charged climate. Consequently, we are truly accepting of few members of our race. Some of us allow our families and very close friends some latitude for the expression of something other than holiday cheer. But for the most part, we keep our emotionality and, therefore, our behavior in check, obedient to the rules that limit the rubric of emotions that are our humanity and our genius.

I am astounded by the human mammal's ability to shut out its own. Given the complicated array of emotions that are involved in all human interactions and shared endeavors, many social scientists, especially anthropologists, are fascinated by the way we maim, blame, and reject each other so easily. Humans are the only mammals who can feel guilt, embarrassment, pride, and humiliation. We are also the only mammals who actually conspire to hurt each other. And none of these complex emotions often induces either side to seek understanding and resolution. On the contrary, they appear to be the very emotions that keep us separate and, if there is a conflict, ensure the entrenchment of adversarial postures and exclusion.

Yet human beings are also supposedly endowed with the critical guiding and checking emotion of empathy. Sadly, the word has, in the last decade, taken on more a linguistic significance than a behavioral one. Recent, worrisome psychological research indicates that this critically foundational emotion is apparently diminishing in all of us.

Empathy is supposed to temper our cognitively thuggish inclination toward meanness. It is an emotive posture that is supposed to make it impossible for us to hurt each other. The equivalent of an electric shock, empathy is an emotion or connection to life that is meant to serve as a behavioral bulwark, the last, unpassable checkpoint before mutual destruction. To put the point simply, I am supposed to hurt if someone else hurts, and vice versa. In fact, the truly empathetic cannot bear either to see (feel) someone else in pain or to cause pain.

Unfortunately, times have changed, provoking, among other things, much discussion in North American courts, in FBI seminars, and among forensic psychiatrists and other mental health professionals about the whereabouts of human empathy. Given the increase in unprovoked physical crimes against strangers or, paradoxically, loved ones, human beings appear to be able to hurt each other more often, more deeply, and more easily than as recently as three years ago.

Further, we are exhibiting a numb indifference to each other in business and social environments. We are, to put an enormously complex issue simply, hurting, judging, and dismissing each other more easily. Eliminating people from our lives or dismissing them for mere difference (ethnic, ideational, and so on) appears to have become as simple and as mundane as blowing our noses. Indeed, evidence suggests that the mere concept of goodwill toward others is, for too many of us, just another seasonal platitude or a sentiment periodically acted on as part of a quid pro quo, implicit or explicit. Merely being attentive to the needs of others is perceived as an impossible mandate.

This phenomenon probably arises partly because we are conscious of and angry about having to shut up about our own needs and pain. Indeed, even our meanness tells a story of shared needs and vulnerability. Like the so-called lesser beasts, we are mean when we are hungry or afraid. And we are both, though tenuously civilized.

Accepting Emotionality

The danger inherent in human beings living too close together and being inescapably mutually dependent and competitive in indifferently ruthless environments is obvious. Yet we continue to perform our frenetic, fear-suffused dance with what some scientists refer to as *devolving emotionality,* a human curse at least as devastating as other natural disasters. If, as some social scientists think, life has become too complicated and demanding for us to feel for and about each other, then we are, indeed, in serious trouble. And the predicament is worse than most of us take the time to consider; fully acknowledging the degree of our passive acceptance of our inevitable misery and evolutionary demise would require too much in the way of feeling and expression.

Our posture toward emotionality necessitates our keeping it to ourselves. We have contracted to attempt to have no effect on each other whatsoever at a time when industrial sages submit that reciprocal, emotive exchange and creative contact are more important than ever. In the name of keeping our emotional waters calm, we live, act, and even speak words in stone-still distance from other souls. This common posture pertains to all life contexts, including what should be creatively noisy work environments and the supposedly validating unit of friendship. This posture—to describe it more accurately, this convenient, self-sustained belief—assists us in avoiding the therapeutic essence of even moderate intimacy and trust, significantly less than the degree of connectedness necessary for both healthy living and new, cooperative human endeavors.

It is strange to read words that seem so impossibly true. We know that we need more from each other and that we have a need to give. Yet from where are we to listen to and hear each other's calls for help, regardless of their form and without judgment? We have to undo the defensive posture of easy dismissal, whether we live in disconcerting times or not.

Simple Wisdom, Sane Solutions

We can hear calls for help and for love if we choose to, even when love and trust seem to be emotional postures of another era. With both risk and daring, we can design and sustain new routes to each other and to new supportive connections.

On a recent US television program, produced and sponsored by the purposeful and sanely driven Oprah Winfrey, her mentor, Maya, a wise, elderly African-American woman, tearfully put this life- and work-related issue this way. "Starting now, with me, there will only be kindness. From my mouth there will only be acceptance, from my lips, tenderness, from my throat a murmuring softness that will speak of my love, not of fear, or of judgment, or of defense. Starting with me. Now. And then you, feeling the strength and safety of my love, will follow."

Maya broke down as she whispered these words to an international audience in spring 1997. She made changing our perceptions sound as wrenchingly simple as it actually is. And it is the only way we can allow each other the latitude we deserve as complex, sensitive, and contemporaneously distressed beings. Each of us has to start by risking—that is, by daring to listen beyond our own versions of what we hear and by responding from a place other than fear or competitiveness. The wars, Maya proposes, the daily ones that are layered microcosms of nation against nation, religion against religion, and the strong against the weak, will stop when each of us decides that there will be *no more* banal brutality among us.

To risk feeling what we really feel is a first step. We must listen to the concerns and note the heartbreaks that have brought us to a place of active, dismissive stupification. We can also benefit from examining the last process or event that turned us away and inward.

I know a woman who remains, in middle age, angry at her still-living father, whom she did have reason to be angry with in childhood. Now, despite having a patient and generally supportive husband, a healthy, brilliant family, a few friends, and her own business, she has a whiplash tendency toward reactivity and dismissal. Without explanation she jettisons people from her life for things that are much of her imagination and that have become unconsciously fused to the anger that simmers beneath her otherwise delightful business personality. She has not, as yet, dared to stop to count her losses or to try to heal. Nor has she assessed the damage done to herself and to people who either cared for or were loyal to her but whom she shocked in personal and business dealings that were ruthlessly dishonest. Her vulnerability, insecurity, self-doubt, and feelings of inadequacy have hurt her and her business. She puts herself at further risk by hiring only people she can control, even intimidate, in order to ensure that she runs the show. As a result, she is inadequately supported, even held in camouflaged contempt, by her own staff.

We are all prone to put together dysfunctional units if we are not creating from a place of self-knowledge and self-recognition, let alone forgiveness. Particularly when holding tightly and resentfully to old wounds, we are infinitely more likely to do harm than good in our endeavors with others. And we are infinitely more likely to self-destruct out of sheer resentment and the tendency to reject. We all need to examine our hearts and minds for heart mines that can detonate, old fuses onto which we hold with the grip of cumulative anger. We need to realize that our underlying emotional postures create both a focus and consistent patterns for our decisions about whom to trust, what and whom to try to control, and whom to hire to support us in our work endeavors. If we were to risk listening to our own thoughts, our vulnerability, and the hurt beneath our anger or disappointment, many of us would realize that we have established situations in which we undermine ourselves and the structures we misguidedly build with stealth and distrust.

By traveling beneath our own skin, we learn a great deal about others. Human beings are so perilously alike that if we do not understand each other, we can live only in defensive conflict. As a mental health professional and as someone honored to work and live beneath the skin of others, I am well aware that too many people remain in caverns they protectively created early in life. Yet risking exposure to the hard light of life is a requisite not only to understanding the misactions of others but also to being capable of empathy and compassion. When we shield our own hearts, we shield much more of ourselves, including the anger that made us turn away in the first place. Only with an understanding of ourselves can we feel beneath and beyond the actions of others.

Unquestionably, some behavior is reprehensible and necessitates our setting clearer boundaries or actually closing the windows to our hearts. However, this measure should be much less frequent and automatic than it has become. Only dangerous behavior of the most extreme kind warrants our judging or otherwise turning away.

Seriously disturbed people are a responsibility of a different kind. They should be guided to places safer than the naively kind hands of novice fixers. Unqualified souls who have a chronic need to take on the mentally ill are not truly connecting. More often than not, they are acting out their own problems related to worthiness, dismissal, and rejection. This extreme and dangerous position ignores truth and is far from what I am proposing here.

In short, people who are destructive and dishonest need to be held at bay and, if possible, led to professional help. They should be loved at a distance, not dismissed through condemnation for they are already malfunctioning from their personal place of self-condemnation.

Understanding, Being, and Letting Go

Everything that we bring to ourselves or that comes to us depends on our ability to let go of anger, fear, and judgment. To judge is to be judged. To fail to recognize a call for help or someone's painful, messy attempt at self-protection limits the expanse of our own psyche and soul. In essence, we join those who are lost when we fail to recognize them as such and merely condemn them to further isolation. Moreover, our own dark spaces become lonelier when we deliberately bar ourselves from understanding the existence and nature of the dark spaces of others.

We are all better off taking the time to sense the life beneath the skin of the magnificently creative and potentially loving creatures that we are. To do so, we use the same complex intrapsychic mechanisms that enable us to become mired in places of dark isolation and misaction. In breaking socially sanctioned, even dictated patterns of dismissal and exclusion ourselves, we learn much about the pain and motivation of both ourselves and others. We also learn about a difficult but intelligently humane alternative to rejection and retaliation in response to human misaction of the socially unpermitted kind. In short, through mere understanding and acceptance, we can both teach and learn new ways of being.

By testing alternative responses to others, we become more likely to seek understanding before or after we ourselves mis-act. Further, by changing our perceptions and by seeking to understand the behavior of others, we learn more about our own potential for reactivity. We also learn how to give to others and to inspire emotional generosity and courage. The gifts of understanding, acceptance, and forgiveness are the just rewards of those who remain vigilantly nonreactive amid the expeditious cruelty that defines socially regulated misbehavior. We can know and let go of infinitely more about each other than we have ever had to or been asked to. Kindness and understanding are still culturally avoidable requisites for surface success and superficial contentedness. We are, however, finally experiencing—if only unconsciously—that without them we can neither work nor live with any depth of satisfaction. And perhaps we will see, as surreal as the idea seems, new cultural edicts about basic human behavior. Imagine there being rules again, as there were in childhood, about how we treat and interact with each other. We really did learn all we had to learn in kindergarten. But we both forgot and ignored it—to win and, more recently, not to lose.

CASE STUDY

A Reactive Businesswoman Calls for Help

The case of the insecure middle-aged woman mentioned in the body of this chapter's text is worth a bit more discussion because it depicts a common but less obvious kind of dismissive behavior.

The woman's business is a small public relations firm, and she and her hard-working but ill-equipped staff continue to lose clients because of unthinking and dishonest behavior that affects clients.

The situation is sadly unnecessary. Were the owner not so entrenched in an angry past and a defensive and suspicious present, she would risk meeting with her staff and revamping how they do business. (She long ago dismissed the suggestion of a mission statement—including values, action plans, and avenues for open communication. It would have required her sharing control and risking real connections with clients and colleagues alike.

Public relations is a people business, requiring solid rapports and loyalties. Clients cannot be expected to tolerate the erratic behavior resulting from this boss's defensive and reflexive inclination to charm and then to dismiss or mislead people, including clients and colleagues. Even her own staff underperform because of their boss's dismissive reactivity—and it shows in the bottom line.

The point of this case study is twofold. First, dismissal doesn't pay. Whether a relationship is personal or professional, reasonable and reasoned behavior is a requisite of sound connections. Not all connections are easy, but managing them is part and parcel of both growing personally and doing business.

Second, the woman's staff do her no favor by merely ducking her moods and destructive, knee-jerk reactions. This avoidance is just a passive version of dismissal. It does her a disservice, and they dismiss her further by discussing her draconian behavior with others outside the firm. Were they, as colleagues, willing to brave a legitimate connection with their sometimes likable boss, they would begin with the risk of honest feedback.

These coworkers have no real connections with each other, and the boss is the primary splitter. She is clearly, through her behavior, calling for help, for understanding, even for someone to stand up to her and set limits. Her clients, of course, would rather move on than have to work at a business relationship. But her staff is another matter. By not connecting with her and sharing truths, they allow her to continue to injure trusting and revenue-producing souls. And they all, the boss included, continue to be hurt themselves.

EXERCISE

Watch someone's behavior today—in a meeting, in traffic, at lunch. Imagine how that person is feeling (not thinking). Then try to feel what he or she is feeling as if it were your own emotion, and note what you feel in your own heart. Do this often, every day. And do not stop because it is painful; if you are lucky, it will be.

Principle 6

Living Lessons

We are all teachers and students to each other. Some teachers and lessons are more harsh than others. Be aware of the lesson inherent in every interaction or relationship in the present as well as in successful or unsuccessful relationships from the past.

How can one learn to live through the ebb-tides of one's existence?...Each cycle of the tide is valid; each cycle of a relationship is valid...and whatever recedes will eternally return.

Anne Morrow Lindbergh

Everyone who has ever related to us emotionally has taught us something. When we think about how we have evolved to who we are, how we are, and what we are in the present, it is clear that each person we have touched or been touched by has given us a gift of self-knowledge. Each relationship, positive or negative, has taught us something useful about ourselves, precipitating the development of previously undeveloped strengths or illuminating previously hidden areas of weakness. And knowledge and growth around our weaknesses is just as important, if not more so, than the discovery and development of our strengths.

For fundamental reasons, the notion of old lessons too well learned continues to crop up amid the principles in this book. Indeed, these principles are, for the most part, about undoing lessons from the past that have resulted in behavior that is either unworkable or downright wrong. The discussion of Principle 5 emphasized that we are both resistant and overcritical when it comes to understanding anything but the expected and strictured behavioral norm. We leave each other in distress because early and ongoing lessons have taught us about danger, avoidance, and noninvolvement. To go against these lessons, usually learned in fear, can be extremely difficult. To get beyond obedience and habituation to active involvement in processes of unlearning and learning anew can feel like emotional-cognitive heresy. But it can help us immeasurably for the rest of our lives.

That we benefit from liberating ourselves by relearning is the essence of this chapter.

The Nullification of Self and Other Souls

Understandably, we tend to view the events in our lives in rigid, self-undermining ways. With respect to relationships, we do as we saw and still see modeled or endorsed for us. Indeed, what we see and have experienced is all that we know unless we have searched for a better, richer way to be, love, and grow. When things go wrong in relationships, as they naturally do, many of us tend to hunker down somewhere in our hearts and psyches. We get stuck in resentment, vengefulness, and pain and reflexively forecast (and induce) the ruination of our once forever connections. We do this to ourselves and others with all our past hurts, misunderstandings, and losses until we have created the emotional equivalent of a tumor that saps the strength from our hearts and blocks expression.

Logical and conventionally responsible to a fault and perpetually guilty, our socialized and acculturated nature does not lead us to ponder, examine, and seek to understand the meaning inherent in things, feelings, and intentions gone awry. Rather, we have been taught and encouraged to lay blame, to sever our connections in whatever way necessary, and to learn from our mistakes—that is, to seize the pain and to further recede into a state of social self-defense.

By so doing, we encode our perceived errors and limitations in our hearts and souls. Rather than really learning and growing, we narrow our frame of reference and possibility and merely live on the spot.

In a way, we both choose and want to hold on to anger related to the past as well as to our historic impressions of individuals and incidents. This vicelike grip allows them to continue to play a role in our lives, even if it is a stunting one. Holding onto, even savoring, the poisonous aspects of our pasts keeps us locked away from ourselves, from loving, and from really learning. Indeed, it keeps us from having to do the immeasurably freeing but effortful work described in Principle 1 regarding self-knowledge and self-acceptance. It also keeps us from having to confront the painful but utterly liberating process of forgiveness described in Principle 2.

In short, gripping the categorized negativity from our pasts keeps us from having to face the awesome responsibility of really living and affects, restricts, and exacerbates the potential insecurities of those around us.

Stuck and Condemned in Time

Moreover, as we learn more about people and relationships, we can, for the most part, safely surmise that individuals and circumstances change over time. How many of us would want to have to account for something we did 20 years ago or a mistake we made even last year? We would be loathe to *because* we have changed. Even if we have not learned why or how we took that false step, we at least try to ensure that things do not go wrong the same way again. We all make mistakes; it is the encores that make some of us more problematic than others. Unless those who have hurt us are in a pathological rut, they too have, in their own way, changed, grown, or otherwise moved beyond their errors.

Of course, as already mentioned, some people do become repeatedly, negatively involved, continuing both to function in ignorance and to do damage. This intransigence, advertent or inadvertent, does not mean, however, that *we* cannot benefit from difficult, even disastrous relationships with them. We can learn lessons about ourselves that are commensurate with the degree of difficulty we faced in an emotional entanglement. And we can do that without the direct involvement of the person or persons who injured us.

Too often, relational wounds are not disinfected with closure and, therefore, do not heal quickly, cleanly, or easily. And we can, of course, use this lack of a tidy ending as an excuse to remain bitter or emotionally retracted. But even someone abandoned without explanation is not precluded from learning, even benefiting, from the experience. Popular psychology has, however, so powerfully programmed us to believe that any healing *requires* a heated or intimate discussion between the parties involved that we are inclined to leave awkward, emotionally violent endings to fester into crippling resentment and an obfuscating sense of self-persecution.

Whether we examine the relational accident or not, we invariably had something to do with our being done unto. Ideally, despite the posture—even the absence—of the other person, we should ask ourselves what role we played in enabling that person to treat us hurtfully or to connect with and then leave us. Whether we have been abused, battered, exploited, lied to, or left, we played a role, and we can learn from it. The comment that "it takes two to tango" is not always meant to be unsympathetic in these situations. We can be mean, and we can be naive. We can want to be a part of something or someone's life so badly that we allow ourselves to be used and abused. We ourselves can also unconsciously use a user. Regardless of the nature of our painful relationship, we are teachers, pointing out our weaknesses and strengths to each other. The same process and principle apply to positive, healthy relationships that induce mutual growth.

In negative situations, however, the only way that we can free ourselves from the trap of leaving someone condemned in time is to find the message in the meanness. If we do not, we deny both them and ourselves understanding and forgiveness and remain distant and inaccessible perhaps for our entire lives. We have to ascertain what we brought to the relationship that contributed to the pain or to the termination.

In brief, the most expeditious way to really learn about ourselves and to face our weaknesses is to examine our roles in failed relationships. Similarly, we can find evidence of our strengths (and weaknesses) in relationships maintained in balance and reciprocal love. In each case, we benefit from the greatest teachers in our lives—those who touch us and whom we touch in awkward, trusting intimacy.

Intimate Transformation

I am always aware that when I relate to anyone beyond the mere surface, *I* change. A truthful, earnest conversation, even with a complete stranger, causes at least a shift in both parties. The exchange, the feelings, and the perceptions that comprise the experience add to and change our emotional and psychic makeups forever, in small or large but always significant ways.

Thus, all interactions, long or short, earnest or formal, can be useful. Some of us remain aware of what we say to others and, more important, what we are saying to ourselves when we are speaking to others. Just as we can learn much from unsuccessful or successful relationships, we can learn much about our real selves (our self-motivating and monitoring inner worlds) by listening to our inner utterances. Our self-dialogues tell us if we are relating from a place of fear, of shyness, of inferiority, or of arrogance. They also reveal our lack of empathy or our reflexive distrust, even our naive ignorance with respect to the necessity of setting boundaries.

In other words, our inner utterances are messages that we can use to learn about ourselves in relation to others. What we learn in conversations or interactions can provide us with critical, stopgap information that if pondered and used responsibly, can preclude heartbreak and future relational disasters. Interactive experiences tell us, at whatever level or depth we present ourselves, what we bring to others in the way of weakness or strength, honesty or dishonesty, a sense of unworthiness or an inadequacy-based need to control. Whatever the information, it is homegrown prescience—a window on the past and future journeys of our hearts.

The Benefit of Early Lessons

I am a much stronger woman because I had a challenging childhood. Yet this difficult beginning combined with the joys, losses, loves, and accomplishments of my later years to form the rich texture of my wonderful life. (I have heard many others claim the same positive outcome in adulthood.)

Moreover, as I have looked back, I have been able to discern the lessons learned or skills honed with others in each stage of my life. Both my early childhood and young adult years were internships in empathy and compassion. I also learned at a young age about the consequences of a lack of communication, about persecution, and about the importance of self-discipline, persistence, and self-directedness. Significantly, I learned that risking my love is important and, even more critically, that love must be expressed unconditionally, with no guarantee of being loved in return. Indeed, as I experienced subsequent external and internal lessons, the composite of my life became the equivalent of a mental and emotional lottery.

Idealization and Missed Opportunities

Unfortunately, most of us were socialized to idealize all relationships—whether they be with imperfect parents, with a series of potential life partners, or with neighbors and colleagues.

We idealize (and too often crucify) backward to our parents, comparing them to a televized, false norm, and we idealize potential lovers and friends according to equally false commercial imagery. As a result, many of us are overflowing with resentment. No one has *ever* measured up to an idyllic TV model. We have false expectations of romantic partnerships that continue to lead us astray toward repetitively painful losses. Not having been taught how to love, we are among the fortunate few if we finally understand that *we* create the situations that we are meant to pass through. We experience, learn from, and then graduate from them to more successful living.

This process makes sense when one thinks about it. Who or what could presume to teach us about relationships and life? It comes down to experience and how we come to perceive it.

Lessons to Learn

Consider your own life—something that most individuals rarely stop to do. It seems that the only time that people ponder who they are and how far they have come is when their lives are threatened or they are, voluntarily or involuntarily, removed from day-to-day routines. Not in so-called normal circumstances do they perform what is arguably the most important task of a living human being: ascertaining, by reviewing the past and examining the present, what they are supposed to have learned or be learning from their interactions and overall experiences with others. Being caught up in the fact that a relationship has failed or clinging to the hope that a current one will succeed is about as far as most people venture toward focusing on their relations with others. Friendships, loving partnerships, and communication per se, they seem to think, are randomly successful or the result of a good fit. Without self-examination, they merely continue to search out and self-intoxicate (for a short time) with a feel-good buzz that has nothing to do with the essence and effort of human bonding.

Think about the relationships you have had from as far back as you can remember. Good or bad, what did they teach you? What can you now glean in the way of knowledge or skill? And if you had suspended judgment and historic hurt and anger, what might the other party have learned from the connection?

Even in your work life, what have you learned about yourself by being with the people you have worked with or for? What are you currently learning about yourself as you manage your present challenges? Golden nuggets of self-knowledge exist in innumerable faces, places, and mental spaces.

Further, what is your current major lesson or challenge? If you are reading this, you must be challenged by and interested in life in general or be experiencing something that is bothering you. Who and what is teaching you, and what are you learning? Is it an old lesson being redone or a new one, positively or painfully useful to your personal and professional growth? Whatever it is, it is something that you are meant to learn so as to move on to who and what you are to be and do in this world. Keep in mind that whatever or whoever is touching, hurting, or frustrating you most at this time in your life is knocking on your door to teach you something. Be courageous and listen. Relationships and experiences, at work and in "private" lives, bear wisdom and can precipitate self-change. They are lessons of authentic learning and growth.

I know what one of my current lessons is, and I am trying to stay with what is, for the most part, an arduous process. I know who my teachers are and what the lesson involves. It is critical to my life and to my ability to continue my life's work. However, to be honest, if I had seen this lesson coming, I would have tried to find a way to skip it or to merely audit it from afar. Somehow, however, life's lessons are presented in just time and are unavoidable. What you *can* avoid—but *must not* if you want to evolve and contribute—is the acquisition of self-knowledge and wisdom. Most people want the gain without the pain. Yet the emotional discomfort they endure in learning is nowhere near the pain accompanying the resentment and bitterness that take root because of ignorance of the reality of mutual instruction.

Students and Teachers for Life

When you and I speak, you are my teacher. When I am teaching, lecturing, or entertaining, I am learning something new each second as I adjust to the complex array of personalities and reactions in the audience. I have learned from the cruelty of others and from their kindness. And neither genre of lesson has been more important or less valued than the other. It is critical for human beings to process each encounter as a positive lesson, a way to learn from and grow as a result of intimacy and interaction. That process also overcomes long-held perceptions of failure, historic anger, and self-condemnation, all of which eat people up from the inside out.

You and I will teach and learn until we die. The lessons will never be over. In fact, staying in place in resentment, in ignorance, or in an isolated state of contented resignation is not living at all. Constant or continuous learning, another popular tidbit of organizational cant, is not just about computer or communication skills or the two-day seminars during which participants passively tick off points reworded from the last non-learning experience. It is about the holistic, integral development of a Self. Historic hating can be processed so as to be historic healing. Similarly, past mistakes can be used to induce growth and to increase the ability to be both safely and authentically intimate.

Know that you have taught others even when you inadvertently harmed or hurt them. Further, take your own pain and put it to the best possible use: to gain self-knowledge and to grow. Forgive and thank your teachers—among them those who have died (even if they left you angry). Be a conscientious student, and learn your past, present, and future lessons well. By so doing, you will be taking fundamental steps toward real selfhood. Also, as a consequence, you will strengthen your increasingly important ability to unite in creative human endeavors and, of course, to love.

CASE STUDY

A Disastrous Manager Becomes a "Master Teacher"

Increasingly, companies are counting on psychological testing to screen job applicants for honesty and to ensure a good fit. But assuming that all is well if the numbers and categories come out looking good is naive.

A case in point occurred a few years ago when a Fortune 1000 company hired a 36-year-old woman as a manager. She was powerful and brilliant, had a great sense of humor, and could inspire others to leap out windows if she so desired. And she was at a good age to be groomed by the company to become a female representative at the higher echelons. Things didn't work out quite that way, however.

After a six-month honeymoon, this woman started to show colors that no one had considered and that could easily be obscured in personality testing. She "hated" people (her word). As far as she was concerned, everyone was a "stupid idiot," a potential cheat, and an abjectly lazy layabout. She gave no one in her department the benefit of the doubt but rather made sure that individuals were put on notice as to their inadequacy and that all employees knew that they were being watched with respect to both performance and dishonesty.

Senior management didn't realize its error for quite a while because it received few complaints about the woman. Employees in her department said little or nothing for a while (except to each other) because she was the latest young "turkette" and had signed a five-year contract. They didn't dare let it be known that they hated her in return. Eventually, a few went to their managers, but without much success. Those managers, although they had also sensed the woman's contempt, didn't dare go to their managers and complain.

It was the chief executive officer who became worried. The first alerts were six- and twelve-month reviews of the productivity in the woman's department. He realized that the low numbers didn't match his vision of this brilliant, new, innovative manager with whom he had played golf, had dinner, enjoyed family ski weekends, and shared the odd after-work drink.

When he spoke to her, she indicated that she needed a new staff (more than 1000 new employees) because the current employees were caught up in old ways and were distinctly dull-witted. The CEO listened but recalled that the same staff had performed 300 percent better before the woman's arrival. He wondered how they could have become so stupid so quickly. He then investigated on his own.

He found that the young woman had poisoned the department with her intense expressions of contempt. She was an angry woman who could hold her anger in check when she wanted to and knew how to customize her personality for individuals when she felt like wielding it, but she humiliated her staff from managers to stock boys and delivery personnel. After enough data and information had been gathered, the firm gave the "turkette" a buyout that would keep her living in high style for five years at least.

Reparations started with the CEO's meeting with the woman's department and apologizing (which went a long way with his employees). He also discussed how one learns from each such encounter. He spoke of his own past confidence in hiring the best and the brightest and how he now found himself reviewing much about what he thought were indicators of both intelligence and decency. He asked the employees to try to come out of their understandable state of embitterment to figure out what this episode had taught them. Noting this could be and must be a positive learning experience for them all, he invited each employee to e-mail, fax, or mail his or her thinking on the matter.

The department healed. In fact, perhaps because of a long period during which the CEO attended to the group and responded to their notes, the workers' performance soared under temporary and then permanent leadership. The young whippersnapper was, they agreed two years later, a lesson in splitting and pulling together.

And they were all better for it. In fact, some of the suggestions made during the healing process were implemented, making the work environment better than it had been before the reign of terror. Furthermore, employee representatives were asked to sit in on the interviewing process for the next candidate—something this company had never done before. (It has now become standard practice.) A great leader had ensured that the poor manager became a positive teacher for and to his employees, rather than a long-term force of destruction.

EXERCISE

Today, note and quietly appreciate your past and present teachers. If mine are reading this book, thank you.

Principle 7

Focus

Now is all we have, and each moment is for giving in some way, love and giving being the essence of our humanity. Daily, consciously, give tangibly and quietly to others.

How wonderful, how miraculous it is to just stand here, enriched in the moment, on the edge of tomorrow.

F. D., first written words after awakening from a two-month coma

The point of Principle 7 is twofold. It involves learning how to bring ourselves back, mentally and emotionally, to the "now" of our lives. It also includes learning how we can benefit from grounding, defining, and finding deep satisfaction in and with our present lives.

Living in the moment can be almost unfathomable, given an existence stretched thin by the tug of war between past and future, not to mention the hectic array and velocity of duties and obligations. So much of modern life requires planning, scheduling, and rescheduling. Yet many of our well-laid plans go out the window as a result of changing circumstances and unforseen crises. Thus, our obsession with tomorrow or down the road rarely satisfies us to the degree to which we so naively commit ourselves. Moreover, as the wise tell us, we *never* arrive far enough down the road to have plenty of time to better love our families, check in with dear friends, or to self-nourish.

Our past is another story, however. As a psychotherapist, I am amazed by how many mental health practitioners still emphasize the past over the present. Of course, our individual history and path to adulthood are part and parcel of understanding who and why we are in the present. But the past receives too much emphasis and deference. Moreover, the psychotherapeutic and psychoanalytic communities give us permission, in a variety of powerful ways, to excuse ourselves from life because of childhood or family dysfunction. Fears learned early in life have brought a large (albeit, usually privileged) portion of the population to some kind of counseling or therapy, which has generally led to more-entrenched orientation to the past. Further and even more powerfully, the media still present past-oriented, antediluvian approaches (from circa 1930) to adult therapies.

In brief, when we are challenged or suffering in the present, the expected and accepted norm is to focus almost entirely on the past. For the past half-century, we have been consistently encouraged and formally socialized to look backward rather than straight into a mirror in the present, to understand and to take responsibility for our actions and our growth.

What's Wrong with Backward, Forward, and to the Side?

This normative inclination to look back and ahead is a robbing combination. It virtually guarantees our missing the actual moments and hours of a life that is supposed to comprise bliss, loss, horror, and enchantment—all in the present. Instead, we practice a highly skilled form of avoidance, allowing our lives to speed by, while simultaneously protesting the loss of our youth. For many, the fear of being old is greater than the enjoyment of being young, the fear of illness greater than gratitude for and enjoyment of good health. Fundamentally, we live looking away, back, forward, and to the side as we worry and fret about what might be but isn't, what should be but probably will not be, and what should have been but simply wasn't. We live as ghosts in the only moments of our lives that are real—the here and now—speeding through what is real and ending with regrets.

The Discovery of Being Here and Now

If we merely hold still and sense the miracle of living a given moment, we are invariably moved and awed by just being alive. The strength and stature of our personhood becomes evident when we stop and "be" in ourselves. We can hear ourselves breathing and feel the persistent beating of our burdened and blessed hearts. And our souls respond with a sigh and a smile, at rest. Too often pushed back and forward and away from the essence of who we are, our senses, our brains, indeed our entire bodies celebrate immediate recognition when we do stop to fully sense a moment. It is our integrated, living senses that unite us with all life, and they are able, in the moment of integration, to mend contortions in our beingness. This can be attained *only* in the present.

Thus, experiencing this sense of ourselves requires that we stop, cease to live in times that do not exist, and allow for the soulful expression and involvement of our Selves.

We have all heard about *living in the moment.* The injunction not to waste the minutes and days of our lives makes eminent sense. However, like other overused expressions, such as *love of neighbor* and *human kindness,* living in the moment feels, most days, like an ideal possible only in a cult environment. We have been conditioned to worry, to fret rather than take action, even to medicate ourselves instead of facing what can sometimes be the pallid face of "now." For most of us, the idea of living in the moment is in the same improbable category as winning the lottery. We view it as something that would be really interesting were it within the realm of the natural order of living.

This reaction seems ironic indeed when we recall that living in the here and now is the norm for all animals. We human beings are the most intelligent mammals, but we are also the most complexly dumb. Other mammals simply and unthinkingly commit themselves to living "now." We, however, are just beginning to understand our complexity and our apparent thuggish hold on the past. Burdensomely brilliant, we are able to live our pasts as seemingly real presents by storing potent data in what scientists once thought was our immutable subconscious. Now, however, we know that we can recode our subconscious minds to catch up with our current circumstances—and to free ourselves to live.

What Is "Now"?

"Now" is a strange and foreign place to be. We have to know it and be in it to get a sense of how to stay in or stray into it more often. Yet what most of us do, hourly and daily, is deliberately direct ourselves either backward or forward. If we are not reliving or reapplying past experiences, consciously or unconsciously, we are worrying about or planning something for the future. The present gets very little of our attention, so we miss being in it and rarely, if ever, catch up to it.

In fact, since we spend much of our time reliving or imagining the past and future, the present does not exist at all for most of us. Our here-and-now has become a work space in which we prepare for sometime down the road, a time we will get to when we fulfill certain responsibilities and complete projects, which, in reality, lead only to more distracting responsibilities and out-of-present plans and preoccupations.

The present cannot exist unless we train ourselves to make it exist. In fact, we have to train ourselves to own it, involve ourselves in it, and to enjoy in it.

Old Lessons That Die Young

I know of no one among my academic or professional acquaintances (most of whom are strained by living oriented to the past and future) who was taught that the present is our lives and that we miss the process of living if we fail to note and savor it. In fact, most of us were trained to just get through time in order to have a shot at enjoying a secure future. In educational systems and many institutionalized religions, we learned that we are supposed to be in a perpetual state of planning for life, not actually yet living it. Happiness, for example, is something we plan to experience later, not now, perhaps not even during this lifetime. (Although some religions teach that we can only really live and experience joy after we are no longer in material form, others have us constantly striving to be deserving enough for a secure present that we will never earn or live.)

No present can exist if we compulsively commit ourselves to creating a future or to fixing a past. Moreover, if we dutifully work to rule with "out of tense" mandates foremost in our minds and hearts, we never reach, feel, or experience the present.

In my work with the terminally ill, I have seen too many weakened individuals learn this too late. Most of the souls I have been with during the moments before their deaths have been without bitterness, but they examined their losses in time and love. Belatedly, many were somehow reattuned to some precious moments previously missed. But they experienced these moments as points in their movement from then to this moment of their existence and then to another place of existence and form. Doubtless, with a knowledge of our impending passage, we acquire both clarity and practical wisdom related to the artificiality of time versus the essence of living. In the few moments, days, or hours when we are face to face with death, we are remarkably sane, and we can still, in a way difficult to understand, redo and belatedly cherish moments missed.

Pressured Non-Nows

Those of us who wish to experience "now" while we are still able to do so have to pass and enforce personal, inner legislation to create a current, clean, and clear place to be in the present. Victims of training and socialization, we face "nows" that are too often pressured, busy spaces, altered states in which there is no time for anything—including time. Many of us have to remind ourselves to breathe, let alone stop to check on a loved one, telephone a friend, or to play (if we remember how).

One problem is that many of us have more work to do in a day than we had in a month ten years ago. E-mail, faxes, and voice mail keep data and demands coming, even in our home environment. With personal and work lives to manage, we live between conveyer belts of constantly emerging duties and challenges, and have no time to finish most or even figure them out. Our "moments" come in the form of collapse at the later-than-ever end of the day—the demarcation point being when the flow of duties has slowed to a velocity we can almost bear to ignore.

Our timeless, productive anxiety has a fascinating cyclical dimension. Many of us need a sense of accomplishment, of having done well at half a dozen jobs. We also need to feel that we are solid, loving contributors to our relationships (or that we have one or two) and to our communities. Some of us also parent in one form or another. In short, the quantity of our work makes it virtually impossible for us either to complete it or to do it with the quality we would like. We are trying to maintain impossible levels of productivity and qualitative standards.

Since we can theoretically do this only at the expense of other aspects of our life (including our community, social, personal, and other fundamental responsibilities), we work harder to try to make more time to fulfill our duties. But the immediacy of technology means that we merely accelerate the turnaround time, thus *increasing* our workload. The conveyor belts speed up, rather than slowing down or maintaining a pace.

Thus, we work harder to work harder and never do get to the other, critical aspects of our responsibilities as friends, parents, and citizens. In consequence, we then work even harder.

Eventually, the never-ending working harder becomes the end in itself, a manic addiction that keeps us from having to face whatever we cannot find the time to address. Somehow, drowning in our work is not as reprehensible as putting aside people and obligations. After all, we are doing work, and it is real. Others can see how hard we are working, and eventually they come to understand, define, and excuse us accordingly. The work becomes our rut and our refuge, our overriding preoccupation and obligation as well as our alibi. It becomes us, and we become it.

Ultimately, nothing in this process is about time. There is no longer time for time, unless we make it a priority—that is, unless we *decide* to permanently compromise our level of production and performance. A difficult dilemma, even a challenge of conscience in our culture. Sadly, most people don't have the time to address it, and they resign themselves to productivity over personal purpose in the present.

It's about Time

As much as we are constantly encouraged, even congratulated, for putting our "nows" aside, we have to figure out a way to schedule them. Being a hard worker has always been lauded. Institutions now demand that their top people work 16-hour days, and the old work ethic has gone through the roof for almost everyone employed.

Many of us still think that we are better people if we work impossibly hard. If we stop to look around us, however, the faces are no longer necessarily reinforcing or admiring. No parent is telling us that hard work is all that matters or that work before play is the only way to succeed. If we glance at the faces we do not have time to really see and love properly, it is evident that many in our orbit are sad and tolerantly abandoned. For too long, most of us have just not had the time to notice—much less to address people and things put aside in the name of "later."

How, Now?

I am trying to take the steps to bring myself back to my life. I still, necessarily, work too hard, but I can put myself in a state of mind whereby, even while working, I am in the moment, noticing the movements and sensory dimensions of the environment and flowing, rather than fretting, while I do so.

I have decided to do this in a way in which we can all begin to recommit ourselves to the present. And it is actually not very challenging.

As children, we were experts at momentary living, without polemics or effort. As adults, we can start by simply stopping periodically, throughout our otherwise accelerated days, to listen to, look at, and touch something we would otherwise have missed. We can go into our imaginations or to a place in our naturally attuned inner world to really study a stranger's face, to chat with a cloud, or to glean whispers from a seasonal wind.

I can still walk my dog and instead of treating it as a chore, make it what it was for me as a child. My dog and I didn't walk then; we explored, trekked, saved lives, climbed mountains, even brought supplies to imaginary troops in no man's land.

That dog and my current one are the best exemplars of bringing excitement to the moment. When animals bump into a friend (almost everyone), reconnect with a family member, or are merely conscious, they bliss out. They model living in the present with complete involvement. They have no idea how to wait, plan, or rehearse for another better (never) time in life. For them, living is right now.

Given their example, I now remind myself more often to stop what I am doing that is out of "now" and allow any living, existing source of beauty in my environment to remind me of my own presence in a moment shared. This technique works, even during an interminable boring plane trip, where the "magic" may be just clouds, below me or enveloping me at 30,000 feet in the air. Wherever I am, I can focus on something connected with me by mere attentiveness and thus be transformed in "now."

Each of us can reap the benefits inherent in the richness of our present life. Meditation or relaxed, imaginative quietness is another way in which we can replace ourselves in time. The precise method used to reconnect to "now" does not matter. What's important is that we stop, feel, sense, and exist for a moment—that we feel our human beingness, otherwise muted and strangled by the infinite grip of cacophonous human doingness.

The incontrovertible fact is the *medical* necessity of applying our imagination and senses to where we are in any given moment in order to know, feel, and experience being and "now." Otherwise, we will just continue successfully or unsuccessfully to blindly run ourselves right out of the already impossibly brief race through the short span of time between birth and death.

Giving in the Moment?

We cannot give to others or positively affect them while we are in a race against our own lives. In order to know what and when to give to whom, we have to be focused and involved in the moment. The needs of others, even needs easily met, bypass our crusted senses while we push our way through our daily processes and frantic, modern obligations.

Indeed, others' needs, as well as our own, are only noticeable and addressable in the here and now. We miss the small but grandly gracious moments in which we can help someone cross a street, assist a stranded driver, find a child's mother in a department store, or pause to compliment a colleague whose contribution has been overlooked. If we are hypnotically focused only on our own meeting of objectives and deadlines, we miss connecting with the people of our lives. And invariably, one way or another, we will lose them.

We are, of course, not the only culprits or victims of this syndrome. Most of the people who do not (cannot) stop to let us into traffic, even if they have to stop for a red light anyway, are not cruel and insensitive. Rather, they are totally unaware of others and of things around them, lost in where they are going or where they have been and thus blind to the moment of mutual opportunity. Those who race past us, insensitive to our pain, are merely doing their duty to the modern god of self-destructive hanging in.

Ours is the brave new world no one foresaw or described. If someone had, we might all have moved to Gilligan's Island. At least we would have prepared ourselves for how to be in the world but not of it as replaceable working parts.

If

If "each moment is for giving" in some way (which I believe is the case, both theologically and practically), what does this axiom imply about our antiquated work habits, our attitudes toward our neighbors and coworkers, even about the time we spend with those we purport to love? What light does this principle shine on new social and organizational perspectives, such as sharing knowledge, cooperation, win–win strategies, and partnership? Is it not eminently more logical, useful, and easier to apply them if we slow down so as to notice—even look for—opportunities to do so?

No one is naive about why these humane concepts have suddenly taken on a more popular corporate meaning and importance: they serve firms well in the global marketplace. However, they also serve us well as individuals who need individuals. Accepting what are merely decent human precepts and using them in self-directed moments of mutual support can only be highly, psychologically beneficial.

Personal applications of cooperative concepts also enable us to make sense of and be personally touched by the practice of shared purpose. The "Play Misty For Me" mission statements written by a few good men between golf games during a 10-day retreat to an ocean setting have, we all know, done little to affect how we function. The wordy corporate niceties are meaningless. Snazzy, even poetic statements of purpose invariably first bore and then evaporate from the mind of the average employee. *Performance* and *productivity* are results of purposeful, personal human focus and application. They are not magically induced or increased as a result of new slogans and revised corporate logos.

In the moments of our work lives (the greatest portion of our lives in general), we can be doing what the human heart and mind are designed to do best: creating, giving, sharing, and supporting. However, we have to slow down to sense the moments in which to do so. While other mammals exist by virtue of rote instinct, we have a choice. We can create meaningful moments defined, for example, by caring and kindness, or we can shut each other out. Similarly, we can create and contribute from the heart, or we can fake our way into another place and time, missing an authentic involvement in the present.

The fact is that even as ostensibly brilliant creatures, most of us are not of much current use to a world that suddenly recognizes the need for applied genius, creativity, and focus, even if we work away the moments of our lives. Nor are we able, until we stop, look, and listen, to make innovative, heartful contributions to an increasingly personal and needy planet.

Not too long ago we could, with pretentious inaction, ask "If not now, when, and if not me, who?" We no longer have the luxury for pseudospeculation. Our moments are sacred. They are also of critical, practical importance to a world that has sped past its organistic ability to adapt to and for the lives for whom it is home. For the sake of our personhood, our mental and emotional health, our financial stability, and our social, global infrastructure, the only time that matters is now.

Can We Live a Responsible Present?

I was recently astounded to read that fewer than 30 percent of 35- to 40-year-olds working in Canada have any financial plan for retirement, despite what can only be called an uncertain economic future. Some analysts infer that this demographic group is happily, irresponsibly winging it in the now! On the contrary, I suggest they are likely good folk who spend money and accumulate in the present so as to intoxicate against its discomfort and responsibilities.

In spite of our fear of stopping and thereby feeling the pain we have been suppressing in order to accomplish our many tasks, the benefits of braking far outweigh the discomfort. In fact, the pain is in the fearful avoidance and cumulative strain of torqued self-denial. When we do face the here and now, we avoid crashing in human traffic where stoplights, stop signs, and yield indicators are lifesaving signals, not just annoying regulators. They make for a clearer, safer, and guided journey.

Responsible planning for the process of life is far from avoiding the present. In fact, only periodically slowing down or sitting in neutral can attune us to what is ahead. Moreover, it is in present moments that we sense the importance of future presents. To plan in the now for a comfortable presence and present later is merely responsible living. Indeed, savoring the moments of our lives now makes us determined to act so as to own them later.

The Integrating Principle

Placing this principle at the center of our life process is a challenge that goes against much of what we have been taught. Yet all the principles in this book come back to making applications and adjustments in the present and requiring that we use that present. Our innate and socialized fear of each other, for example, diminishes considerably when we stop and actually look at and sense someone we would otherwise fear in our defensive, adversarial rush. Also, if we stop to think about what we are doing and how we are doing it, we tend to dislike ourselves a little less, strive less fearfully, and, by virtue of refracted projection, judge those around us less harshly. We can, in contrived momentary coasting, perceive others as more than mere impediments to our progress and security. Sometimes we can even feel the potential for souls nurturing souls—in rich moments in a shared place in present time.

A Personal Postscript

As I was writing this manuscript and coping with 18-hour work days to administer a multitude of personal and professional duties, someone I loved and admired was dying. I wanted—no, I needed—to say good-bye to her. And if I had seen her again, nearer to the end, she might have asked something of me, even for just a laugh, as was her inclination, regardless of her physical discomfort and moment-to-moment struggle to stay alive. But I couldn't or didn't stop in time to put in another call.

Late one night, on a layover after a five-hour flight, I picked up my voice mail. Amid two dozen requests for program facts, invoices, scheduling information, summaries, outlines, biographical material, arrival times, speaking confirmations, publisher's queries, and more demands for speedily communicated travel arrangements for far-off engagements was a message simply saying that this hearty soul was gone—and had been for two weeks. I sat, musing over moments maniacally mismanaged. And a few stray tears smudged and smeared the edges of notes made earlier that day.

When the sun rose, I was still in my coat, at my desk, trying to remember who to call back and why. And I had no idea what time it was.

CASE STUDY

Greg Realizes His Need for Focus

A businessman who had been coming to me for counseling arrived one day in a particularly bad frame of mind. He was an ambitious 40-year-old, doing quite well in a new job, which he had decided would be his "big score." The week before he had been worried about doing a presentation to prospective clients, and he launched into telling me the results.

After the presentation was over, his senior manager had told him gently that "something" had been missing. He had all the facts, all the interconnections, even some darn good new ideas, but something had been lacking from the point of view of selling to a client.

In ending the conversation, his boss had said, "Maybe you need to just relax and enjoy your own material." My patient was confused.

After some questioning and chatting, however, he realized that while he was giving his presentation, he had never focused on what he was talking about at a given moment. Instead, he was preparing his next point and checking for audience reaction. What he finally understood was that because he had not intensely, enthusiastically focused on each of his points, his presentation lacked punch. That's what his boss had been trying to tell him.

Any public speaker *must* be in the moment. Audiences have a low tolerance for speakers who disappear, even for a second.

Indeed, no job is done well if our minds are wandering to other tenses and places for any reason. All forms of communication require that we speak and attend to the listeners in the "now," rather than speculating about the results of our performance.

EXERCISE

Today, stop, look, listen, and sense in at least three different environments. Note the newness of the familiar, whether it be a look on a child's face, the posture of a friend at work, your own eyes, or the quirky, jerky observations of a bird on a limb.

And telephone a friend. Try hard not to miss your todays or getting to say goodbye. It is easier to induce and enjoy a smile than to try to remember one.

Principle 8

Detachment and Rationality

Do not cling or grip anything or anyone. Letting go is the most important life skill.

That which is in living essence, whether it be in the form of a visiting bird, a loving partner, or the fading fragility of leaves before they drop away with the seasons, can only touch us if we allow them to leave us. To try to own or to bend beauty is to automatically destroy it.

Anonymous

We have all, at some point in our lives, been convinced that we loved something or someone in a way that no one else could, even when the relationship was unsatisfying. But most of us found out, usually very painfully, that we were clinging to someone, trapping him or her in a way that ultimately stifled whatever degree of love had existed.

Unfortunately, in our culture, *love* often means *ownership* or *fusion*: that two people are melded together so as to be indistinguishable as separate, unique, and vital personalities. This expectation, concept, and warped reality of love as proprietorship are intensely propagated in modern western culture. We grew up hearing the message, even in music, that we are "half, not whole" until we catch and trap a partner. Then we are to settle down as one (and stop growing as individuals). Too often, that settling down really means that two people cease to be as attentive to, affectionate with, or even interested in each other as they were (or pretended to be) before the culmination of the hunt.

That depiction of romantic love may sound outdated or cynical. In most people's private parlance, however, we still hear major implications and even outright statements of a belief in fusion, ownership, and mutual possession and control. In spite of the inordinately high divorce rate and the current propensity toward serial marriages, the baby boomers and the next two generations appear to believe in a partnership paradigm circa 1950, generated and regenerated via the media.

The commercial and political dimensions of this propaganda aside, a large part of the North American population is still working or failing at perfect love. The majority of those under age 50, married or unmarried, are still searching or longing for perfection in a mate with more energy than they use in virtually any other aspect of personhood. The search-and-seizure syndrome—the need to find and consciously or unconsciously entrap another human mammal—is still the defining drive of too many of our lives.

Unquestionably, this drive makes the acquisition of possible mate material all the more intense and insane. With no time to work at a film noir version of *Father Knows Best*, *The Brady Bunch,* or even *One Long Hot Summer,* we are still working our mental and imaginative butts off to find and secure this impossible, illusory dimension of a well-positioned life.

Part and parcel of even nascent success in our search for a temporary-forever, perfect-if-fixed love is the clinging syndrome—a posture defined by a sense of possession, ownership, and hanging on. Clinging or gripping raises its ugly head, first romantically and then, to various degrees, in mundanely dangerous ways. Again and again, I witness the beginnings of high-octane romantic relationships and then their sad and messy endings. I watch as clinging becomes squeezing, manifesting itself most seriously when one member of the partnership attempts to leave or receives the attentions of an outsider. Even if an individual no longer covets a partner with whom he has temporarily settled, he resists (sometimes violently) letting go or giving away what has been part of an emotional and material estate. In short, what we call love—what we have been taught that love is (more so by the media than by our partnership-weary parents)—is too often competitive, conditional, and ultimately cruel. Beginnings bear no relation to middles or endings. Passion routinely turns to contempt if not based on a mature love.

To love someone is to want to be with her, to stand by her side, to share day-to-day experiences and frustrations, and to honor, celebrate, and enjoy the other's individuality. That definition holds in all environments and situations, not just romantic relationships. This genre of mature, imperfect love is at the core of loving communities: families, offices, schools, and marriages. It involves less clinging and more work, less vigilant possessiveness, and more trust than immutually illusory connections.

Yet we have little experience in the how-to of successful relationships in general, let alone of intimacy and long-lived romantic love. Many of us, as immature and insecure producers and consumers, have developed insufficient personhood to trust our own value, worthiness, and lovability enough to form mature relationships. Consequently, we play games, advertent and inadvertent, and endure the posturing, the false intensity, and the often violent disappointment that comes with a game gone bad. We all need to be held, not trapped. Yet many of us still mistake one for the other, in both our giving and our receiving of what is essentially material and medicinal love.

Real Love?

Somehow, partially for reasons already mentioned, we humans fear what could be called *open love*. Our feelings of inadequacy and unloveability are so strong that once we have caught someone, we are damned if we are ever going to let that person go. And if, for any reason, the partner wants to leave us, the so-called love can turn instantly to active hate.

Understandably, the passionate need and fitted fantasy can and do too frequently turn into real primordial rage. For a person who is consciously or unconsciously self-rejected to be rejected by another is the psychological equivalent of being torn from life support. Moreover, with separation comes the revelation of the artificiality of the love and of the fantasy once tacitly agreed to by both parties as the very basis for the union. This, too, is unbearable for us to have brought to the fore by time and familiarity. The shared fantasy of a false perfect love is supposed to be maintained. But built into that fantasy is the danger of a kind of mutiny, of one party's dangerously abandoning the other.

The hunger most of us have for an impossibly infinite connection with another is real, too real to play with. And it forms and detonates more relationships than any other human need. The need is historic, but its current depth and dimensions are deeper and greater than in generations before when, ironically, "love, marriage, and children" were a given. Today we have a greater need to find safe places in other people in order to mask epidemic feelings of inadequacy and insecurity. The objective is to fall in love, to let go of one's self and one's challenges, and to submerge them in flowing or forced but frequently unreal feelings about another. We all need each other, and we feel our needs more than ever, given the strain modern life places upon us. However, we are, sadly, even more prone to look in the wrong places for comfort. We still look for a false version of perfect partnership—even perfect employment—and ever-lasting romance as it is portrayed in a TV laxative commercial.

The Need

The need to feel safe is both normal and understandable. Most of us are walking around with tightened jaws, holding back the anxiety associated with isolation, loss, and anger. So nothing could be more natural than unconscious (even conscious) wishes for an impossible return to infancy, when all was taken care of. Indeed, at the foundation of gripping behavior in relationships is fear of a repeat of the first major loss of our lives—the loss of oneness with mother. Off-the-scale, passionate, romantic love, untested by time and familiarity, is frequently a way, for at least one party, to go home, grow young, and be safe. Safe sex is lasting sex. Otherwise, it is a pitiable version of the suckling for which we all long and which many unconsciously bring to the early intensity of love.

As adult children, we must rationally recompute that we did not let go of mother: she let go of us—whether we were ready or not. For those of us who have never understood this fact of early separation, connection with possible mate material can be immediate, distorting, and irresistibly intense.

The distortion and intensity are hangovers from the early days and weeks of our lives. The immediacy or instant intimacy stems from the unconscious fear that we will never again feel safe and fully loved. And our fragile psyches, for the most part untested in true partnership and personal independence, feel that we must.

In brief, our need to fuse completely with another compounds the cultural edict to live in romantic twosomes. And the currently exacerbated need to fuse in the comfort of blindness and infinite safety is a form of defensive regression. Few if any relationships can sustain such a burden.

Gripping and Other Escapes

For similar reasons, some of us, at one time or another (usually during a break from the search-and-seizure syndrome) turn to other, safer, yet still often spurious commitments. Many baby boomers, while faithfully antichurch, are "doing" spirituality. Many of us claim oneness with all living things, while still keeping half an eye and half our sexual energy open to false romantic possibilities. We continue to grip the notion of the perfect love, even while we commit ourselves to having that regressive and protective perfect rapport with a deity or with groups sharing a common addiction, recovery, or cause.

Ironically, those of us with an inclination to cling are running in place, like frantic wanderers, well-dressed nomads pretending to be everything we are not. We seem fine without that perfect love we both want and loathe because we don't have it. We are not fine, however, and we know it. We know that if even a temporary love escape from reality and responsibilities were to turn up as a mere possibility, we would grab and grip it in a second and, with preconscious, sweet, blind naiveté, vow to never let it go. On some level we know that we are in a holding pattern, waiting for this to happen so that we can place it in some safe, inaccessible corner of our scary lives. Then, and only then, that secret, misleading part of us tells us, we could get on with the other, seemingly less important aspects of our personhood, such as creating, designing, and living our lives. But, many of us still think, first things first.

In my private practice, I see just as many bright, competent women and men who are still waiting to get to their life's work at age 50, as I see individuals struggling with family, work, and stress. In a way, even though finding any mate is a tough challenge these days, it is still, for many, a raison d'être, a priority ahead of solvency, accomplishment, and other extracurricular interests. The can't-be-alone syndrome is a deterrent to solid relationships and to overall accomplishment. In short, it is a lifestopper.

The Consequences

The inclination to cling and grip exists well before we can either stalk or trap a mate. Throughout our lives, we have a tendency (unless we deliberately grow out of it) to find something—a partner, a dedication to a group, a commitment to an ideology, even a dedication to a place of work—that we can hold on to and use as a diversion from the complexity of selfhood. And we move from one grip to another with a frightening split second of suspension in between.

Thus, we place great if unspoken onus on our new handle. If that new person or affiliation fails us—that is, fails the test of our prefab, customized fantasies or fails to meet our exposed and intensifying needs—both we and the object of our clinging are in serious trouble. Clinging, a lack of intelligent detachment, kills. The inevitable fall from grace is destructive to both sides. Whenever we tuck ourselves under an imagined arm of infinite safety, we are setting two sides up for a messy no-win situation—all in the name of love or promise.

We have all seen couples who came together with good intentions and are now bitterly apart. And many are as sane or saner than we are. It is not that we are crazy. It is that we are blinded by a version of love and partnership that is virtually impossible and likely to explode. We are victims of the bombardment of imagery about perfect, sexy, no-demand, no-work love. We don't understand that it doesn't exist, not without time and mature, mutual acceptance.

We also don't comprehend the dangerous and heartbreaking ways in which we need and want this fantasy. We seek it to fill all our empty, injured spaces. Perfect love would, we assume, quell our own feelings of inadequacy and fill the desert of modern life. Yet nothing that we create in our imaginations and grip for life is going to soothe us. Neither our new cars nor our new lovers seem to care for us for long. And, the truth be known, we tire of them. We make fun of the fact that we fill ourselves up (for a few hours) when we go shopping. And the first question a friend asks amid a hiatus in relationships is "Have you met someone?", not "What is interesting or fulfilling in your life?" Many of us find nothing left to talk about except the renewal of the search; only a minority discuss the complexity of family, children, sustained love in marriage, and a life's work.

The preoccupation with self-distraction in precarious unions excludes other untapped dimensions of life and selfhood. It is a certain symptom of empty hearts and unconsciously self-limiting minds.

Clinging through Boundaries

The latest trendy, "live-withable" disorder is codependency. Everyone speaks of it, and everyone pretends to both understand and avoid it. Yet most of us have at least one codependent relationship in our lives, and most of us do not die from it. (I have an irrefutably codependent relationship with my dog; she is not the least bit worried about it, and neither am I.) Mutual need, even unanalyzed and undiscussed, is normal and fine. In contrast, codependency, in its clinical form, is a direct result of our positioning our needs and our intentions so as to be symbiotic with the false or positioned needs and intentions of someone else. Codependency involves gripping, usually speed gripping, to get it started, and its relationships are based, albeit innocently and ignorantly, on a mutually agreed-upon denial of both real needs and real selves. They show up later—just before the protonic splitting.

Smothering a relationship with an impossibly fantastic definition is also about a lack of boundaries. To let someone be who he is, we have to allow him living space. As individuals, we need space to be, to create, even to have a separate and growing personality. The tendency to smash or to emotionally seduce our way through boundaries—with someone else's permission or before she knows what has happened to her—is pregripping, pre-codependent behavior of the most genuine kind. Being blind to boundaries is as much about being blind to one's own real needs as it is about being blind to those of others. And it speaks loudly and mournfully of disappointment and loss, all in the name of obsessive, forced, and entrapped intimacy.

Freedom to Love

We are back to self again. We cannot love if we do not know what we might bring to a union that is not love. We must also be gently aware of the fact that human beings can project hurts, injuries, and the emptiness of a lifetime onto others—all in the name of falling in love. And such a fall can be of huge proportions.

We do not love if we do not love freely, and we are not being loved if we attach conditions to the purported love or if the other party does so. Love has to be open, or it does not exist at all. If we cannot loosen our grip, we are not loving; we are caging. Letting go means simply letting someone else be herself to do what she needs to do and allowing for the vagaries of separate identities. Freeing someone else to love or not to love instills in that person both the will to love and its antecedent, the ability to trust. Without the skittish, unconscious sense of being in a bad play whose tragic denouement has not yet been written but will be, we can achieve growth and love.

Approaching love from the perspective of a false, fantasized belief system is much more difficult than enduring the messy reality of loving negotiations between two imperfect Selves. The latter is safely if painfully sane. In successful life partnerships, each person is free to feel and to express, to have space and individuality, and, therefore, to stay and to love.

Trusting that beauty and real affection will stay in the form of romantic love or companionship is difficult for many of us. And it has become more difficult as shaky North Americans seek solace and comfort during a period of pandemic insecurity. Short of lashing people to chairs, we have all, at some time, held on to someone too long and too hard and either lost or injured him.

It is better to learn about the nature of love and its freeing quality and then to set out, in Self, with an appreciation of boundaries and of other imperfect hearts. Then we *allow* love to come into our lives. Truly, when we do grip or trap someone, what has love got to do with it? Ultimately, pervasively, and painfully, the answer is nothing.

Detachment and Work

By necessity, this section has focused on our approach to romantic love and to personal relationships in general. However, our search for perfect, safe places and spaces does not preclude those places in which we earn income.

The 1990s brought immeasurable trauma to seasoned workers used to the notion of lifetime benevolency—even entitlement—regardless of the value an individual added to the environment and bottom line. For many years, our institutions, especially our bureaucratic organizations, had promised a lifetime of paychecks and demanded little in the way of independent input. Until very recently, blue-chip companies held the promise of undemanding, desultory security. Thus, today, as companies increasingly act on new mandates for production and excellence (real commitment and hard work), entire employee populations are in shock. Merely staying in place, playing it safe, and showing up for 20 or 40 years is no longer enough in work environments of integrity. However, the safe haven approach to job and career is still the approach most deeply imprinted in the minds of employees of all ages. The rapid and polar transition from collecting a paycheck to having to make a creative, cooperative commitment is an enormous leap, and for some, an impossible one.

The safe-haven approach has much to do with our inclination to cling to what appears to be secure. We not only resist change. We do not know how to change or, indeed, how to become employable—that is, to develop skills and talents that can be tailored to various positions and projects. Moreover, we were never taught how to continuously learn and develop new skills (we were just suddenly told to), and most people doubt that they are able to do so. In fact, most employees have difficulty merely understanding the concept of ongoing learning, let alone accepting and acting on the edict.

Yet the basic need to feel safe, secure, valued, and liked does present a potentially positive aspect for employers. If they understand and benevolently exploit basic human needs, there is fertile interpersonal ground from which to teach, both through example and through patient recognition and acceptance. I have seen rare leaders (not necessarily managers) at work. Whether or not they know it, when they are successful at bringing the majority of an old-school employee population up to speed, they are meeting fundamental human needs and inclinations. A leader, male or female, inspires loyalty, even absolute devotion, if he or she provides an environment of emotional safety and commendation for employees. A model of strength and consistent fairness has an almost hypnotic effect on even the most cynical of populations. Ironically, this powerfully motivating and integrating approach has more often been associated with cult leaders than with leaders in either industry or government.

We probably will not all be sufficiently fortunate to encounter such enlightened leadership in our jobs. But the fact remains that we can no longer become traditionally attached to our places of work. Even the expectation of office space—symbolic of employment identity—is archaic and naive. With the advent of virtual offices, we can no longer expect to find special spaces in the work club to which we go each day with the pride of membership. We have to adopt new ways to work in virtual, home, and mobile offices of increasingly varied and distant kinds.

Moreover, and more pertinent to our need to learn detachment, we can no longer simply identify with who pays us. We have to commit ourselves, as the best and brightest, to whatever we are doing and for whom we are working at any given time. The rewards have changed, and the accolades are more personal, portable, and consistent with independent self-discipline and growth. In this new era, to cling to the expectation of a status quo is to have missed the fact that our organizations and institutions are being revolutionized. If there is a new *status quo,* it is more aptly labeled a *status grow.* From one day to another, nothing remains the same, and security is a process of ongoing self-creation, re-creation, and intellectual and emotional growth.

Trust and Letting Go

Gripping—even searching for something or someone to cling to—is, more than ever, self-defeating. Unchangeables do not exist, even and especially among human beings. And now, suddenly, in our lifetimes, our social structures are changing more quickly than the seasons.

Although our gripping inclinations are exacerbated by rapid transition and loss of environments, people, and loved ones, we have no choice but to work at this aspect of personhood. An opportunity to fill out as human adults is upon us. But we do not have to frantically search for anything. All we need, both to share our lives with integrity with another and to succeed in new and newer work places, is to develop the self-respect, self-confidence, and adaptability that come with growing up strong. To be healthily, successfully detached, we have to cling to and commit to a secure, lifelong relationship with our Selves.

CASE STUDY

Andrew Learns the Hard Way about Clinging and Control

The following case study is particularly for this section, but it is also the saddest case in the book. It involves a man who clung to both his marriage and his work until he lost both.

When Andrew's wife told him that she wanted him to leave, after 24 years of marriage, he begged, wept, nagged, and eventually talked her into going to counseling with him—although even he knew that therapy was a stopgap measure to give him more time to figure out how to convince her to stay married. When the counseling simply made it clearer that the couple no longer had anything in common and should separate, Andrew became exceedingly irrational. Otherwise a gentle man, with no history of abusive behavior, he kept coming to the house, swearing at his wife in front of the children, telephoning the children and telling them that their mother was trying to destroy him, and harassing her at her place of work. The situation became so bad and mutually humiliating that his wife obtained a restraining order.

Concurrently, Andrew's company was undergoing massive changes to keep up with technological advances and product development. Even before his problems at home, Andrew had been looked at as definite buyout material. He was set in his ways, not very good with people, and used to long lunches and short days. When several senior managers finally confronted him at a planned meeting, he flew off the handle, threatened to sue, told them they were "bastards," and generally swore his way out of a letter of recommendation.

Six months later, with most of his termination package spent (and some put in trust for his children), Andrew vanished. To this day, no one is sure what happened. The assumption is that he committed suicide in the ocean on the west coast where he had lived before the separation. His sailboat was found, but he was not.

Andrew had clung to wife and family for identity and safety, not for reciprocal, mature love. He had also used his work to create the only supporting identity he had. Family and work made him feel safe and real, and without them he had no identity or sane sense of self.

Ironically, in disastrous romantic relationships, the rejected mate often kills the rejecter. In this case, with all lost, Andrew removed himself. If he had remained detached, with a strong, separate self, yet loving and maturely devoted, he would have had both his family and himself to lean on when crises befell. If he had been an independent and evolving Self, rooted in his own livingness (and enjoying and sharing that of others), he would never have been faced with the same challenges. What defeated him was the inability to develop an independent self and live without the only defining external supports that he had.

EXERCISE

What are you clinging to today? Is it a relationship, a problem, a job, or an object? Ascertain how this posture is serving you (and others in your orbit), and consider loosening your grip. Practice not needing anyone or anything for one day, and write down your feelings after so doing. Those feelings will be something you can own, learn from, act on, and build on. Continue to let go of—or give much space to—these things and people you love and enjoy.

Principle 9

Peace over Conflict: A Choice

Choose to be peaceful inside, regardless of circumstances. When you let go, just know that all will be well. Save for creative action energy you could devote to conflict and adversary.

Inner peace comes from both the acquisition of self-knowledge and a sense of belongingness and safety in the world. It is maintained by remaining of human environments, not in them.

John Murphy

Many people doubt that we can actually *choose* to be peaceful. Most of us do not know that we have a choice about how we experience all circumstances, as well as how we react to other people.

Our doubt about the idea of being peaceful is compounded by our having been trained, early on, in conflict and adversary, rather than in harmony, cooperation, and grace. To fight things out was the norm. To walk away from a bully without rising to the challenge was perceived as an act of weakness. Boys and girls alike, we learned in elementary school, for example, that reporting the poor behavior of another child and asking for help were regarded, more often than not, with mild contempt by both peers and teachers. This was not the case if we stood our ground, allowed ourselves to be bullied, or fought back. Parents varied in their messages, but other children and other adults were usually inclined to have us fight, rather than snitch. And the media clearly and consistently encouraged a good punchout over peaceful resolutions.

Moreover, although we were encouraged—but not shown how—to communicate and to make as many friends as possible, we lived on red alert. We were taught to be prepared for that which is threatening, rather than to be open to that which is soothing, friendly, and good.

As adults, we are barraged with reminders of a plethora of random acts of violence. How can we be peaceful in the environment in which we live? When fear-driven manipulation, dishonesty, and cruelty are depicted so commonly as to become the promulgated behavioral norm, how do we find peace? In this rough reality, how can we actually choose peace over vigilance or conflict?

The Search Outside

Inner peace is an extremely rare experience, though it need not be. I am saddened to think of the thousands of North Americans who feel they have to make expensive treks to faraway places to find inner peace. They go to meet far-out individuals who apparently—and sometimes do—possess special wisdom, focus, and attunement and who guarantee what has eluded these folk for a lifetime: mere peaceful contentedness. Not necessarily religious people, these seekers are on a voyage toward someone (or something) whom they believe can give or bring them lasting inner peace.

Yet although some souls can profoundly affect us, even amid our daily routines, if we are open to them, real, lasting peace does not come to us as a result of external influences. Even the powerful influence of a modern-day sage cannot, in the intermediate or long term, transplant inner peace into untended inner worlds. There is no McPeace, a microwaved version of contentedness to be brown-bagged and ingested. Rather, peace is a rare, intricate, and personalized commodity of and in oneSelf.

The genre of work described in Principle 6, whereby we allow others and experiences to teach us, is an example of the kind of work on oneSelf that allows for inner change and peace. Others can teach us much about behavior and introduce us to the tools of self-excavation. A few can even provide, by their mere presence or feedback, a catalyst for a long overdue inner shift. Inner peace, however, is a gift given to our-selves by ourSelves. Like love, happiness, success, and good health, peace cannot come from someone or somewhere else, regardless of our level of influence or material riches.

The Element of Choice

Inner peace is itself a choice. If we ponder the implications of peace-fulness, we have to conclude that attaining it must involve, to varying degrees for various people, a regular drawing away from the magnetic hubbub of modern, daily activity.

Choosing peace does not mean that we have to leave our jobs and be-come cave dwellers. It does, however, mean that we make a commit-ment to removing ourselves, as often as possible, from the normative politics of everyday life. And doing so requires that we become aware of how we feel and what becomes of us as we participate in our life envi-ronments. We have to remain in conscious, inner dialogue with our-selves (a condition elaborated in Principle 13) to avoid getting caught up in swirls of tension or negativity.

Merely noting how we are affected by what is going on around us de-mands a choice and perhaps even a sacrifice or a calculated risk. To step away from toxicity or adversary is to become uninvolved with people and processes to which we may have become addictively attached—indeed, to which we may have been clinging for partial self-definition. We also run the risk of missing something: facts or data that we do not want to forgo and, more important, do not want others to have unless we have them too. In that most of us do not trust others to share knowledge, re-moving oneself, even for moments, from the fray requires a major deci-sion and commitment. However, the psychological gains that accrue to us from backing off are infinitely greater than the petty losses. We gain mental clarity and stamina, not to mention increased overall physical re-silience, from regular periods of peaceful detachment.

Being peaceful does not, of course, mean spacing out. It is mental removal, not anesthesia. We can tune out whenever we want to, and we can just as easily tune back in. In fact, as children, we traveled in and out of mundane realities regularly. And we still do so as adults, albeit rarely and with less ease and natural, imaginative comfort. In fact, we are suspicious of and nervous about peacefulness. It seems to be entirely unproductive. Nothing could be further from the scientific truth. Our cultural disdain for anything considered unproductive has killed as many active contributors through heart disease than have obesity and cigarette smoking combined. Regular periods of peace make us healthier, stronger human beings (among other things).

Stillness

The way to peace is *staying within and doing without.* We should not, however, attach traditional, paradigmatic meanings to the instruction. In particular, *doing without* does not mean necessarily sacrificing anything material. (In fact, those who have learned to focus peacefully usually tune into and attract abundance.)

The directive actually refers to the fact that we have to go within—do our inner work first—in order to make successful applications of our Selves in the outer world later. At the very least, we can perform our daily duties concurrent with a process of ongoing inner awareness.

Regardless of strategy, we have to spend some time in peace within ourselves to be balanced and focused and to perform positively, productively, and creatively in the spinning outer world. We need to maintain an inner equilibrium and do our lives from beyond, transcending the tunnel-visioned hurry-scurry of western human environments.

In fact, whether one strives to contribute or to merely get through the day without a headache, a commitment to working on inner grounding or peace is a requisite. To search "without," whether it be around another person or through the accumulation of material objects, is futile. The outward search itself is dissonant and repelling of peaceful people and forces.

Many years ago I realized that no one and nothing else could provide me with a sense of peace, so I started to work on creating periods of stillness—creative, motivating, propelling, interpretive, and leveling states—in my inner world. Since then, I have become increasingly sorry for those who approach modern life without this critical inner tool. It is especially disheartening because I know that the positive benefits of peaceful interludes are cumulative. The sooner we start to incorporate them into a daily schedule, the sooner the benefits become significant and measurable. Feelings of greater relaxation and well-being, as well as increased creativity, are noticeably greater in as little as two weeks. After a year, our day-to-day living can feel profoundly different. We find we are able to accomplish more and have increased endurance. Peaceful people are successful, regardless of how one defines success. For one thing, precisely because they are peaceful, others are attracted to them and follow them with ease.

Many years after my initial commitment to quiet myself, I still spend much of my teaching time encouraging successful North Americans to regularly retreat and go within, to imagine a peaceful experience and thus replenish themselves mentally, emotionally, and physically. This way, their success will be sustained and their resilience in the face of constant millennial challenges maintained.

Further, I am incredulous that our educational institutions have still not introduced this critical skill to children and teenagers. In fact, in most elementary schools, silence is still used as a form of punishment, implying naughtiness and exclusion. Most teachers have never experienced the benefits that accrue from the ancient and now critical life tool of peacefulness. They, like most parents, teach scramble and competition, not quietude and monitored self-growth.

Many of us who regularly induce the relaxation response are surprised that the eruptions and random acts of violence are so few, given the state of unenlightened tension that can define and help to direct our lives. However, in most "advantaged" human environments, numb indifference has set in, and that is more pervasive, even dangerous than open, discernible violence. Instead of our circuitry's blowing, it hums out, dimming the light and colors of the human soul and thwarting individual emotional and sensory awareness and creativity. Without retreating and retuning, we end up with little space for active doingness, let alone orchestrations of the soul.

The mind-soul-body triad is too great to mismanage without its falling into crisis. As complex beings, we need inner management at the best of times. Strained or not, we must stop acting so as to manage the integration and mutually responsive components of what is meant to be a peaceful, thoughtful state of being. The chaos, the mixed messages, the technological threats, and the human complexities are more than our untended psyches and bodies are able to handle. We need to employ a few counterbalancing exercises daily in order to go at life with any degree of consistent intelligence and productive sanity.

Thus, many physicians, especially cardiologists, are now publishing books based on teaching people (primarily highly stressed and highly paid male executives) to acquire and maintain inner peace. This critical state of mind and body, necessary for sustained performance, is a strategic removal of self from the cacophony of human doings with other human doings. Systematic removal allows for self-nurturing and self-resourcing in a state of focused stillness. The results, in the short term, are greater calm, increased resilience, and accessible, cumulative genius. In the long term, they are greater creativity and the solid grounding that comes with physically and mentally tended Selfhood.

Exceptional People

Top athletes know the importance of cultivating and exploiting the benefits of inner peace. Just before a race, for example, competitive downhill skiers recede into themselves, whether it is to merely settle and prepare the mind-body for the race or to visualize their win before the event.

Jimmy Connors, Tiger Woods, and Sylvie Forechette all know and practice creative, preparative stillness to focus and posture themselves for competition. But John MacEnroe, probably once the most talented tennis player in the world, neglected his inner world and performed little inner training and preparation for a match. And in competition, he repeatedly lost his focus (and his income and place in tennis history) because of his neglecting this most motivating and directing of mental dimensions.

The old expression "the loneliness of the long distance runner" is often misunderstood. Most long distance runners are not lonely at all. They are alone, focused, and able to bring mental acuity, an unstrained cadence, and competitive stamina to a current challenge and to subsequent endeavors. If this cumulatively clarifying and productive focus is *loneliness*, we should all be so *lonely*. The misleading word actually refers to resourceful communication with that dimension of our neurophysiology that is most directing and encoding of integrated success patterns. And the natural cadence of running, brisk walking, or swimming while simultaneously emptying the mind of all external worries is a fundamental way to address success.

The Peaceful Side of Success

The new fortune-makers are at rest, most of them practicing daily exercises in quietude. A minority of baby boomers with new ideas, self-knowledge, cultivated creativity, and a will to act are coming up smelling like both roses and money. Some of the old-guard senior managers have also trained in the art and science of creating and exploiting the cumulative benefits of inner peace. Business schools are including in their curricula a variety of ways to learn the composite skill of removal, relaxation, and focus. Doing so is both good business and a key ingredient of sustaining excellence. A large number of highly successful corporate leaders and sales superstars have learned to incorporate this healing and honing skill into their lifestyles.

Peacefulness has to be scheduled into our routines. Countless people have told me that they do not have time to take the time to be peaceful. I sympathize with both the perception and the reality, but I can respond only with a tiresome admonishment: we have to find and make the time (as we eventually do with our bodily functions), even if it means getting up a little earlier, shortening the ingestive portion of our lunch hours, or interrupting reading, work, or television after dinner.

We have to do it, just as much as we have to breathe and consume water. Given a guarantee of an exponential increase in sound productivity and ease of performance, we would be self-destructive fools to ignore the long-known, scientifically proven benefits of focused, imaginative silence. No longer just an eastern or esoteric phenomenon, it is sound, accredited medicine for sane living. Without it, studies show, our mind-body systems function well below what they should and can, and the chances of falling ill with one of the numerous lifestyle diseases is substantially greater.

Avoidance

The older we get, the easier it is to apply and benefit from the skill of stillness—and not just because those over age 50 are more fatigued. The older manager or employee has seen it all and has less to prove than does someone who is climbing the corporate ladder, trying to keep (or find) a job, or more inclined toward manipulative deflections than self-direction.

Moreover, as we creep into our middle years, we begin to question the efficacy of much of our socialization and programming. Fast-track doing is eventually not enough. And it certainly does not assist or maintain inner peace. For some, this discovery comes too late. Just doing has made the years fly by faster, the moments invisible or unaccounted for.

Just doing is the undoing of the essence of human life. We are meant to create and to absorb the many facets and textures of life and to leave a semblance of our intangibility as part of our legacy. Yet in modern western culture, most of us have time for none of these things. Those few who do stop periodically to reassess, to redirect from within, and then to revise their actions and involvements accordingly, live infinitely more satisfying lives.

It is from within that we maintain perspective, develop confidence, and objectify dreams. The power of real contribution comes from tending to our lives inside out, from focusing and then taking action in the material world. Soon our inner and outer worlds work together to guide us to design and enjoy a life in which we are living, creating, and loving Selves.

The Extraordinary Ordinary

Every extraordinary person I have ever met, from Bobby Orr to Vice-President Al Gore, has practiced some form of quietude, directed relaxation, or meditation. Indeed, the change in people who incorporate a version of strategic peace into their routine is extraordinary. They become creators and contributors, not just in their work but in various dimensions of their lives.

Most people who have worked this natural magic into their lifestyles did so initially as a form of stress management. Some adopted the practice twice or three times a day to improve their performance at a sport or to increase their stamina on the job. All, however, soon realized that much more than increased relaxation and improved performance came with exercises in stillness. Cumulatively, they became smarter, more mentally agile, more sanguine, less impatient, and more insightful and creative.

In other words, much that gets squashed when we are caught up in "rev states" (the racing-rat-in-the-maze syndrome) is liberated by simple, cumulative, deep relaxation. In fact, studies show that IQs rise from one year to the next as a group of people practice strategic stillness. Social-interactive, sales, and management skills all increase significantly after a short period of regulated practice with inside-out self-management and growth. Using psychological terminology, one can say that a result of cognitive cessation, myriad talents and modes of expression are found in and liberated from the subconscious and preconscious. By practicing peacefulness, whether it is of a passive nature (just quietude) or dynamic-directed (used for planning and rehearsal), a talented hockey player becomes a National Hockey League all-star and a violinist ends up playing solo at Carnegie Hall.

And by being regularly peaceful, we too can cease to be ordinary. *Ordinary* is an expression (or the result of the expression) of external reactivity only. As a consequence of directed quietude, we can draw from stored wisdom and imaginative capacities otherwise unavailable in the superactive yet paradoxically stunting left brain. *Extraordinary* combines the vast capacities of the human mind and spirit with externally applied talents, strengths, and abilities. The contemporary heroes of the baby boomers—Ted Turner and Bill Gates, the first trillionaire in history—

are not banking on good math or planning skills or a half-decent degree. They create, contribute, and profit enormously from the practiced, strategic use of a well-tended and implicated inner world.

Peace and Principle

In this attenuated period of social relativism—the pervading theme in the courts, in social work, and in the mental health professions for decades—someone finds an explanation or excuse for any behavior. Yet right and wrong still exist, whether or not we recognize or pay any attention to them. Choosing peace can help us to clarify and find our way through the times' ethical labyrinths.

Psychologists and neurologists alike find that when individuals regularly take the time to be peaceful, still, and deeply relaxed, they tend to be at ease with and comfortably self-trusting of their moral and ethical postures and decisions. Further, because they are comfortable in their own skin, they have less difficulty making judgment calls and doing the right thing with respect to others.

This response is merely the natural, only thing to do, given their sense of their relationship to others, as well as their monitored relationship to their own inner world. Most people have forgotten the notion of principle-centered leadership, one of hundreds of late-20th-century organizational fads that sounded great but didn't work. Principles, ethics, decency, and consistency and congruency of behavior are unlikely to be put into regular practice after a peppy one-day seminar. They come automatically only from a sound, secure, and ordered inner world, the place where real connections, concerns, and caring have their roots.

Understandably, those who commit themselves to daily, positive quietude become infinitely more empathetic. Indeed, although doing the right thing does not always ensure that no one gets hurt, peaceful people find it virtually impossible to cause undue pain, to exploit another person, or to subject someone to an injustice. The connectedness among us is clearer to those who regularly spend time peacefully exploring their inner worlds. In the environments in which they administer, their decisions are based on human and humane perspectives, the direct opposite of the reactions of those who work in fear with externally driven reactivity.

Thus, without buzz phrases or announcements, individuals who are peace oriented are automatically inclined to be consistent and congruous in the application of basic ethics. They take a fearless, mature, and creative approach to people and projects because they are in touch with a center—one, scientists submit, that we all share. Behavior increasingly common among child-adults who function in a ruthlessly hard shell of presumptive entitlement are unfathomable to those who, by being in touch with their own inner worlds, understand the needs, fears, and complexities of others. Those who have a place to go within themselves and nothing to fear from themselves or others have no need for conflict. Nor are they tempted to resort to mendacity of any kind.

Peaceful souls can also admit when they are wrong, partly out of respect and empathy for others wronged and partly because they are open to learning. By virtue of cumulative self-knowledge and self-respect, those who choose peace do not need to close doors and to deny. Nor could they. They have become sufficiently connected with life itself to be at ease with it, as well as with the complexity of human dynamics and the vagaries of individual behavior. They are exemplars of the words *mature* and *sane*.

Peace and Work

Analysts offer irrefutable proof that choosing peace in the workplace virtually guarantees the creation and maintenance of a contented, productive workforce. When entire employee populations perform one or more exercises a day to still themselves, to renew their focus, and to increase innovative thinking, organizational climates change. Studies also show that those who manage their inner worlds—who feed the integrated dimensions of their Selves with automatically increasing periods of inner peace—are more resilient and productive in otherwise stressful work situations; they also have better overall human relations, reflecting problem-solving abilities and conflict management skills that are well above the norm.

Management benefits exponentially from introducing this mind-body exercise and posture to the daily activities of employees. Even when just an organization's managers learn to mentally stop, they eventually manage in a more enlightened, insightful, and effective manner. Self-attuned, peaceful leader-managers are powerful models who induce, almost immediately, positive changes among the employees with whom they work.

Even the best manager undermanages and underfunctions as a leader unless she opens up the various dimensions of the mind that can be liberated by purposeful peacefulness. For reasons already mentioned, a manager acquires the powerful nuances and sustained force of leadership by accessing qualities that transcend the rote codes of conduct presented and accepted for years as appropriate principles of practice and performance. Sound management is one thing; effective leadership is a horse of an entirely different color. Leadership, many people now argue, exists only among the very few who quietly bring to the task and the responsibility the talents, insights, and innovations transcendent of mere cognition.

Moreover, no one leads efficiently until she has acquired a natural inclination toward and a commitment to peaceful creativity over paralyzing conflict. This is not to say that a true leader becomes fearful of conflict. On the contrary, someone working from the inside out does not need to use conflict as a tool and comprehends its dire effects. Creative conflict is essential to working organisms. Conflict among the fearful or nonparticipating, however, is seen for what it is: a serious human and organizational problem that can kill performance and bring toxicity to an otherwise healthy environment. Under enlightened leadership, it gets fixed, benevolently but efficiently.

Peaceful Nonactivity

Everything we do and are is affected by how peaceful we are at heart. All versions of the practice of inner peace stress that it is not about doing at all. Rather, it is about stillness resulting in inner and outer security and benevolent and beneficial self-managed behavior. Those who are internally peaceful—that is, those who do not live in a world of what-ifs, historic anger, fear, and suspicion—attract good people like human magnets. The human mammal can sense legitimate calm in others, and it is immediately comforting and freeing. We know when we are safe with each other and when we are not. Unconsciously, we know when to totally trust another and when to do so would be dangerous.

We have all experienced the latter situation. In fact, most of the patients I see as a psychotherapist believe that not trusting anyone is the norm, and most of the audiences I speak to across North America feel the same way. They find it hard to swallow the idea that there exist certain peaceful people who can be trusted. Peaceful self-confidence in a dissonant world is virtually impossible to accept as a possibility, let alone a necessity. Conflict, hidden agendas, and criss-crossing scheming, even among one's closest colleagues and friends, are somehow easier to expect.

We have all been burned by lost souls stupefied by the struggle to make it on one cylinder—that is, without the propelling support and direction of a solid, mature inner Self. Too few of us, however, have met and dealt with true, unambiguous goodness, especially as a component of success. We attribute goodness to rare souls such as Mother Teresa, and we assume an overriding inclination toward dishonesty among each other. No one has taught us either the importance or the immeasurable value, intangible and material, of choosing peace. Subsumed in action, conflict, fear, and ruthless competition, we are blind to inner peace, the essential ingredient of successful living. Right there, within the same mechanism that drives us everywhere else, lies the contract awaiting our commitment. Choosing to be, to think, and to act on peaceful solutions over common conflict is to create inner and outer environments of an integrating, salutary, and nonerosive kind. It is a choice that promotes life, creative contribution, and abundance of all kinds. It is also one definition of sanity.

CASE STUDY

John and Adrian Choose Peace over Multiple Losses

John and his wife, Adrian, both in their late 20s, decided to work seven-day weeks to jump start their business. They very much looked forward to having children but wanted to ensure that they were solvent first.

John was the real powerhorse. Even though he spent most of his working hours either angry or frustrated, he was incredibly productive. Adrian was also remarkable in terms of what she accomplished in an 18-hour day, but she became ill more often than John did. She always seemed to have a mild cold, a sore throat, aching muscles—something that made her feel less than 100 percent.

Adrian usually got home around 10:00 p.m., and John would arrive home anywhere between midnight and 3:00 a.m. Sometimes he just slept in the office and changed his shirt in the morning. So Adrian was not surprised when her husband did not come home one Thursday night. She called the office, left a message on the voice mail, assuming he was in the outer office and didn't hear the phone, and went to sleep.

It was the superintendent of the office building who found John that night—within minutes of his having suffered a massive heart attack. The super, who often came by when John was working late, found the 27-year-old slumped back in his chair with combined terror and agony on his contorted face. He was starting to turn blue. The superintendent called 911, performed CPR, and saved John's life—for the time being.

To make a harrowing story short, John underwent major surgery, barely survived, and was hospitalized for three months. He was then in rehabilitation for a year. As cardiologists are increasingly seeing, John had an enormous explosion of the heart, even though he had no history of heart disease. He simply worked himself sick, whipping, admonishing, and pushing himself like a cruel animal trainer. Moreover, he was always worried, even frightened, about whether he and his wife would make it. He had started to take minor obstructions personally and to have at least one major tantrum a day, throwing papers and swearing up and down that the world was out to get him. Yet, his emotional reactions aside, he had been highly productive. Adrian was also a worrier but had managed her temper and attempted to help John manage his. For the most part, when he had become angry and irrational, she had just given him space.

The heart attack changed their lives—for the better. Now, as part of the cutting-edge therapy related to recovery, both John and Adrian have learned to manage their inner worlds, especially the messages they send to themselves about their successes, failures, and priorities. Each also takes three time-outs a day, in solitude. They breathe deeply, imagine beautiful scenes, and "sense" sunlight and soft breezes on their faces. Due to their inner work, they have learned to function with EASE (effortlessly applied sane effectiveness).

Adrian is pregnant, the business is doing well, and neither John nor Adrian will ever again treat themselves like mechanical mules. They have also grown to depend on their times of self-mollifying and replenishing quietude. As they were told, it helps them to feel peaceful and cumulatively enables them to deal less stressfully with long hours and day-to-day problems.

They now give classes one night a week to other entrepreneurs who would otherwise also be working in a state of fear, strain, and, inevitably, conflict.

EXERCISE

For 10 minutes, stop what you are doing, take a few deep breaths slowly in and out, and use all your senses to experience yourself in a perfect natural setting (of your creation or from memory). When you emerge, slowly count yourself up from one to ten. Note how you feel. Do this at least three times a day, and write down how you feel after a week.

If you are a manager-leader, encourage others to do the same. Then, after about two weeks, note the change in the environment. You will find a marked decrease in tension and noticeably improved performance.

Discuss the principle at a meeting. Ask each person to comment after reading it. A shift will occur merely by virtue of the fact that someone dared to suggest that peace is valuable and that more benefits accrue to humans from being than from just doing.

Principle 10

Life Design

Continuously set goals, and daily go slightly beyond what you think is your limit in relationships, in service to others, and in your life's work.

All our lives are unsweetly short. But to live without purposeful accomplishment guarantees that our last moments will not only be characterized by a fear of the unknown, death, but also by a striking terror—the fact that we missed our own lives.

Ralph Waldo Emerson

In the long and short term, life has to be lived on purpose. Most people who live accidentally are unhappy, lack enthusiasm, and envy others. In fact, those who do not think about, mentally create, and note on paper a virtual blueprint for their lives are significantly prone to a variety of physical illnesses as well as to the postindustrial epidemic conditions of depression and anxiety.

Over and over again, I see reminders of the need for life planning in the lives of others: from a bright and hardworking government employee trapped by pension-building at age 50 but wishing that he had used his talents elsewhere, to a searching 28-year-old without any sense of direction for life at all. Without applying fundamental mental-imaginative skills to the art and science of living, we all risk being burdened with unsatisfying existences. It thus behooves us to learn the skills of choosing and planning a life. Otherwise, living is just a haphazard experience punctuated by birth and death. And in the new millennium, the experience of life unmonitored may well be a flash and then a mere blur in black, white, and unremarkable shades of gray.

Focus by Default

Having known the duress of the Great Depression, many of our parents and grandparents think their youth offered little latitude for choice and planning. But they did have, by necessity, an intensity of focus. Although based on the fundamental need to eat and provide for dependents, it allowed many to discover, push, and direct themselves early.

This is not to say that the Depression assisted that generation in finding their life's work (although, in some cases it did), but it does say something about incentive, simplicity, and focus. Many of those who innovated, working themselves to the bone during those hard times, and then further succeeding because of what they had had to learn about directed persistence, admit to being pleased to be removed from today's workplace. They profess to having been boggled, at the end of their careers, by the chaotic insanity of a world suddenly defined by transient needs, ever-changing priorities, and fundamental insecurity.

Most members of this large demographic group worry (for their children and grandchildren, as well as for their own security) about the seemingly closed and demanding nature of the current and future job market. Today, work environments appear to have no room for trial and error and no stable barometer of success, while the room for failure seems enormous. Most of the very people who are to feed an increasingly weighty social support system are paralyzed by what appears, to the older worker and manager, to be a multiplicity of nonchoices. Thirty years ago, individuals chose a career and worked hard to become a secure success. But we are not in Kansas anymore, and the Wizard's little black bag of clear answers and directives no longer exists. The young, emerging members of today's work force, as well as those who perceive themselves as trapped in a day-to-day organizational flux, have been given no idea whatsoever as to where and how to apply themselves to make pertinent changes in how they work and live.

For some, the ante is not yet sufficiently high to try. Many potential workers prefer to wonder and wander, rather than to experiment with personal innovation and risk. Still buying into the traditional notion of security, these young and not so young candidates for contribution are still waiting for something to open up in the once benevolently cozy confines of overstuffed private- and public-sector organizations.

Ironically, obedient, linear thinkers face both too many inaccessible choices and an insufficient need for their services. The average secondary school graduate has already learned her lessons too well. And sadly, what we learned to learn about life and work has little application in the actual practice of life beyond graduation. The inadequacy of the curriculum aside, no one told us that we would have to both create our own lives and work at happiness. Most certainly, no one taught us to seek out and attempt to apply our vision of who we are as individuals to our presumptuous expectations of being automatically successful workers and professionals—a notion powerfully inculcated by the overnight acquisition of medical and legal degrees and automatic multinational corporate power and wealth as depicted in TV fiction. No wonder several generations are both stunned and angry. What we learned provided no preparation. And what we saw was insidiously and stupefyingly demotivating.

Choice and Life Design

Unfortunately, almost no one except John Kenneth Galbraith and myself mentions Herbert Marcuse anymore. A once much-quoted 20th century philosopher and social scientist, he predicted the difficulty inherent in entering a society and an infrastructure that would be so varied and in sufficient flux as to make the average enthusiastic graduate blanch. He predicted a society with, on the one hand, a virtual monovision regarding financial security and success and, on the other hand, so many and so few ways of acquiring this success that the multiplicity of choices would be paralyzing. As a result, many candidates for social participation would find themselves lost in impossible possibilities.

Marcuse's paradoxical vision is upon us. Increasingly, we hear people say, "Hey, I've given up looking for what I really want. Now I'll just settle for a steady job!" Yet there are no more steady jobs to speak of and, for the vast majority, no perceived alternatives. To assume the existence of fallback positions within the rubric of traditional assumptions is to have missed the shift.

The challenge—indeed, the prerogative—is no longer about choice but about creativity, risk, and applied personhood. It is also, inescapably, about a process whereby we revolutionize the way we see ourselves in relation to income-producing activity, whereby we question specific assumptions and expectations about effort, commitment, and the boundaries between who we are and what we do.

In a new and healthy way, our work and our essential character must be in consonance, either fortuitously or by mental design. We can no longer send a nonthinking, nonfeeling, protective fraction of ourselves to productive endeavors. Nothing less than a holistic approach to work will do. Indeed, "value-added" is merely self-added, the commitment of more of our unique individuality to our endeavors and to our alliances with others.

New, creative applications of our talents and our Selves are both much in demand and much rewarded. As already suggested, what we have been taught in school and social environments is about as useful in the current employment market as having learned to plant daisies on the ocean floor. Thus, too many of us perceive ourselves as unwanted, unworthy, and inadequate, and if we do hook something, we watch over our shoulders for signs of elimination—hardly the ideal psychological posture for innovation and creativity. Yet we have virtually no one to copy. No tried and true "get through the day looking okay" technique exists anymore. Talent and input, then more new talent and input, and then still more comprise the peripatetic process and theme of today's work.

In such an environment, authentically accessed and applied character necessarily triumphs over the superficial, unchallenging application of personality. *Character* brings with it involvement and is constant and creative. *Personality,* the strategically changeable outward expression of who we are, is tantamount to inadvertent fraudulence, a superficial substitute for the in-depth application of a real Self. The right personality used to pass for most-likely-to-succeed; now its use applies only to short-term gains by the conscious or unconscious manipulations of a con artist.

Clearly, someone must at least inform a confused population of the new requisites for success. Mere employment in a hirer's market depends on new and inordinate applications of ourSelves to both task and environment. Those who try to find work in a country that continues to support those who have stopped trying do not understand the new prerogatives. We are well into an era that has no room for grunt work but demands greatness as manifested in the application of personhood, regardless of the task or the position. Job level matters less and less for participation and contribution. The custodian of a school must be as familiar with its credo as the principal and the teachers. At a large corporation, the support staff must be as familiar with the corporate vision and current strategic direction as are the vice-presidents.

No position is secure, or is any job description static. Those who learn to plan and to apply their Selves, their essential and unique character, to a design for work and life will soar with increasing agility. They will also have benefited from a period in history when "individual growth and development" is no longer a pleasant platitude for outdated, yet colorful training manuals. It is and will continue to be a requisite for employment and successful living.

Practical Purpose and Meaning

Places, positions, and projects that require both character and talent, not to mention creative hard work, are now the norm for employment opportunities. The same goes for our income-producing lives in general. We have to do more with ourselves and our lives than we were taught or ever thought in order to access, sustain, and direct ourselves so as to end up in an acceptable place now, as well as down the short road to old age. The new and ever-changing demands of the market have resulted in our having to do two things: first, find out what we do best and position that talent in the right place at the right time in the right way; and second, create and manage a life.

Critically important to designing a life (as well as to becoming and remaining employable) is a sense of purpose in our impossibly cluttered lives. Too many people think that an epiphany in childhood is the only way to acquire a life's purpose. On the contrary, we can ascertain *at any point in our lives* why we are doing what we are doing in the way, place, and organization in which we are doing it.

If we cannot think of a meaningful reason for what we are doing, we have at least one major explanation for our malaise and overall sense of discontentedness. We are missing critical components of a living life. My dog needs no life plan nor vision to chase her ball or to hang her head out the car window; neither does my cat to sleep, eat, or take up the better part of a king-size bed. Purpose and vision are, however, fundamental dimensions of our humanity. Whether we are consciously aware of it or not, we need a sense of meaning in order to search for meaning and to establish meaning in our lives. And to establish meaning, we need to be both human and spiritually and mentally healthy.

A large part of the malaise and exogenous depression that suffuses much of the western human community is symptomatic of the fact that the struggle to be able to earn and consume has become our only purpose. This raison d'être is lethal for human beings. We are, in spite of our thuggish dormancy, spirited and passionate beings. With no reason to live beyond planning to shop on our day off, we are undermining our godliness and relegating ourselves to the dependent role of the passive observer. We are also, as studies show, sitting ducks for various forms of "dis-ease" by virtue of what has been a gradual atrophy of the mind and spirit.

A Personal Mission Statement

For managing our performance and creative contribution, each of us should have and be guided by a personal mission statement—a PMS.

A PMS should specify: who you are; what kind of person you are and behave as; how you would like to be remembered after your death; what you do for income, and how much you earn; what and how you contribute to the community in a nonmonetary way; whether you have a family, and if you do, its size and the values that unite it; where you live (geographically, structurally, and so on); what you do to remain fit and energetic; and anything else that's important to your being *you*.

A PMS must be written in the present tense, not in the future tense. If it is written in the future tense, it might as well be a wish list, and, as we know, we are a population of frantic if cynical wishers. Thinking, even planning, entirely in the future fails to create an "I-am-ness" and an ownership of the present and future moments of our lives. We cannot commit ourselves to an attempt at life design if we are unable to say that it already exists as possibility as part of our present. Ultimately, the only way to bring about the material reality of our personal vision is to believe it and live it as if it were *now*.

By the time we are in our mid- to late-20s, a PMS is a necessity. It is the equivalent of a life map, with long-term destinations clearly defined and with much of the how and when taken care of. Writing it forces us to compute consciously and subconsciously where we will end up and how we will feel upon arrival and also who and how we will be along the way. The objective and the process are equally important.

A multitude of studies show that human beings fare significantly better if they have a vision and a life plan of action and objectives. Those who merely flow through and out of a mandatory academic sentence or who choose to work but do so with resentful indifference fare remarkably worse in all aspects of life.

What a rude awakening to discover that neither academic credentials nor stagnant employment provide a guarantee of successful living. Life as we know it is indifferent to those who have not yet decided what they will contribute and how they will do so. A plan, passionately committed to, attracts the support of what can be called a life force. Energy attracts energy, enthusiasm attracts enthusiasm, and creative persistence is rewarded with opportunity. Moreover, people are attracted to people with motive and momentum. We like to be around them, to attach ourselves to them, and to share their energy. The charisma of the lifemaker is actually the energy emitted from someone who thinks about and lives a directed, managed life.

On the other, more common side of the coin are talented, even hardworking people without plans. Those of us without purpose are like animals who stray from their natural terrain. We wander—listless, directionless, confused, and then broken in body and spirit—to nowhere. Human beings are creators and doers, and unlike animals, we need the punch of passion to live full lives. The passion related to contribution, to the ideal of making a difference, small or large, in the lives of others, is the greatest propellant for successful living. It is also a constant in an ever-changing formula for success. The passion of purpose enables us to progress amid the multitude of mixed, mandatory incompletables that scatter the landscapes of our lives.

The obvious reason, therefore, for writing and committing ourselves to a PMS is to provide ourselves with a personal sense of direction and a transcendent purpose. When circumstances beyond our control become extraordinarily chaotic and unpredictable, those of us with a PMS remain unflappable. Instead of merely worrying about vocational future, mortgage payments, and position power in a specific work setting, we have an overall, overriding sense of purpose to measure the mess against who we are, where we are going, and what we have done and will do that is fundamental to our life purpose.

Human beings with PMSs are exponentially less likely to break under the strain of global, organizational, and even personal change. We have vision, a purpose, and the drive and excitement that accompany them. Most of those without a *formal* PMS or a commitment to transcendent purpose have no foundational buffer in the face of changing circumstances, individual malevolence, personal loss, or daily disappointment. They have no reason to get up, brush themselves off, and keep going after a bad fall. Nor do they have any reason to stretch beyond their historic limits to create new and higher ways of being and doing. Whatever happens, a PMS allows us to bring personal meaning, continuity, and constancy to otherwise uncontrollable, human, organizational, and global variables.

One final point is worth noting. A PMS can be written at any time in life *except* childhood. A plan provides pressure, and we have all seen the often bad effects of pressure on children to succeed in a certain profession or to a certain socioeconomic level. Too frequently, it backfires, leaving otherwise capable adults frozen in the headlights of potential success and failure.

Childhood is for mucking about, dreaming, being unafraid, experimenting, and discovering abilities. The greatest gifts a child can receive are a feeling of safety, a sense of value, and a groundedness in the world. All serve the adult later in organizing and designing in accord with a celebrated, acknowledged, and self-respected individuality—outgrowths of having been intelligently loved.

Fortunately and necessarily, as adults, regardless of how we were maintained as children, we can and should reprogram in accord with who we are, separate from our beginnings. Our pasts, good or bad, are no excuse for either a sense of entitlement or for limited living. If we have not met with success, we have the cognitive tools to change both the historic theme and the objective conditions of a previous life. There is scientific proof of the efficacy of new beginnings.

A Personal Tactical Plan

A serious, working, living PMS has a related personal tactical plan (PTP). Again, studies show that individuals who attach action steps to their objectives invariably reach their goals. Then they are in a position to set new and higher ones, all related to a PMS that is constant but flexible. They are what I call *easy risers*.

By remaining focused and in control of their destiny, they are continually reaching their goals and discerning and designing the next step, for which they raise the bar automatically. Early on, having learned the grace of accomplishment, they come to see no other way to live.

Such action-oriented individuals, in or out of organizations, do value-added work and, given their drive and flexibility, are forever employable. Self-starters, self-managers, self-motivators, and self-directors, they reach goals with relative ease and are inveterately alert for new, related, and greater opportunities.

Individuals who have this life skill are miles beyond the norm. Yet they should not be. They have merely caught on to something we all should have been taught well before it became an urgent requisite for success and well-being. They are exceptional-normal human beings who can make and keep commitments to life, themselves, and others. They take chances without fear and live life with creative, excited anticipation. They are, to themselves, to their families, to institutions and corporations, the exemplars of freely, creatively involved beings—and, as such, are worth their weight in gold.

Best or Beast

As complex creatures of thought, imagination, passion, and intuitive connectedness, we are capable of both miracles and acts of shameful malevolence. With no consistent, overriding guidelines or goals, we merely live day to day, fearful, erratic, and exceedingly quick to judge. Left to our own random devices, we are much more likely to manifest the beast in us than to perform uniformly beneficial miracles.

In order to achieve sane success (a clear and deliberate redundancy), we need the steadiness of reason, the cushion of meaning and objectives, even the dreams that come with thoughtful self-evaluation, self-definition, and planning. Unfortunately, the word *dream* is often belittled. Here I use it to mean something at which we are aiming and with which we are living day to day to bring it to fruition. It is the psychologically and spiritually better place in which and by which we choose to live. Further, a dream in action tempers and integrates our complexity, making us less fearful and much less inclined toward conflict or facile meanness. A dream with a plan also keeps us challenged, with a reflexive will to raise our sights. When wrapped in the framework of a PMS and a PTP, distinctively human energy propels us to higher, better living.

The nature of the human beast is that we need to be challenged, rather than to be merely accepting of or beaten down by circumstances. In North America, family conflict, breakdown, even domestic homicide are on the rise, as are suicide rates and substance abuse. Afflicted with loss of hope and absence of active dreams, much of the population lacks energy and basic contentedness. Our hearts and minds—our inherent genius—demand that we bring integrated meaning and direction to our lives. (If we do not, history has shown that someone else will.)

Planning and writing a PMS and attaching a PTP are not parts of a process we embark on solely for the sake of our work, socioeconomic expectations, or even a specific interest or activity. They are components of a personal infrastructure (foundation) and suprastructure (attitudinal posture) designed to include personal relationships, our service to others, and our personally defined relationship with life and creation. Further, they are to calamitous change what cockroaches are to nuclear radiation. They cannot be damaged or destroyed—regardless of the power of the blast.

Put simply, planners are better people. They have the latitude to be. However, they are, as yet, a minority. Unlike the well-trained and well-strained majority, they are sufficiently involved in their self-directed responsibilities that they are usually noncompetitive, noncombative, nonreactive, and easily cooperative individuals. They have no reason to withhold information or knowledge or to wish for the failure of others. Nor do they need to hurt or impede others out of fear for themselves. They are intuitive doers, rather than insecure, advertent, or inadvertent destroyers. They are in place and going places as self-respecting Selves.

The Sky—and Beyond

Ambitious young people used to be told, "The sky is the limit." If the sky represents the old limit, then the new one is further off in the galaxy. And we can take ourselves wherever we want to go with the right planning and the right guiding purpose. The plan allows for—indeed, requires—what I call *blind courage* or *faith*. Along with persistence, courageous belief is a mental and emotional posture that takes us, on good days and bad, through the sometimes meandering steps planned for our success. Our personal sense of purpose can also keep us on track ethically and morally. It enables us to be conscious of the needs of others in relation to our own intentions, actions, and accomplishments. Our sense of purpose in a human community of shared hearts and souls keeps us clean, not mean, and vigilant against injustice. It also ensures that we return as much as we acquire through intelligent living. Giving back becomes as automatic and as mundane as expelling borrowed air.

Studies show that most present-day working people do not like either what they do or the current state of their lives. Too many of us find daily life a drag. As a psychologist and social scientist, I believe that this sad fact results from a lack of goals, objectives, and a reason to live, as well as from feelings of worthlessness and inadequacy in a weird new world. We need to self-renew by attaching concrete, personal requirements and objectives to our lives, thus allowing for a daily sense of significance and accomplishment. Planned, impassioned, directed living can turn mere subsistence into an ever-exciting process of human creativity and growth—with no time for wishes-become-regrets.

CASE STUDY

Twins Set Contrasting Life Objectives

Psychotherapists are fond of talking about a case that you may have heard before. Twin brothers were born into a family in which the father was abusive, alcoholic, and chronically unemployed. From their early childhood, he beat them frequently, often severely enough to render them unconscious, and he sporadically abandoned the family.

The boys grew up to be almost converses of each other. One became sadly like his father. He was a serious alcoholic, lost his family, could not hold down a job, and was known to settle differences at home and elsewhere with his fists first. At the time of the study into the twins' lives and backgrounds, he was close to death at age 38.

When asked why his life had turned out this way, he looked at the interviewer with dismay and said, "Obviously, because my father was a drunk, he was abusive, he didn't work, he abandoned us, and he died young. What did you expect my life would be like?"

In contrast, the other twin grew up to be his father's opposite. At the time of the study, he had a wonderful wife, two loving children, and solid good friends. He worked for a large bottling company and was promoted until he became its vice-president and then president.

When asked why he thought that his life had turned out so well, he said, "Well, obviously, my father was an abusive drunk, he didn't work, he abandoned us, and he died young. Seeing this, I never wanted to be like that, or to have my wife or children suffer the way we did. So I planned, early and throughout my whole life, to ensure that this would never happen to me. I made sure that I knew where I was going and what I wanted. I stayed focused on what I could do and be. Wouldn't you?" he asked, as if the answer to the original question were obvious.

The main difference between the twins was one of choice and then of focus, perspective, and design. One, hopeless and broken, randomly fell into what had been modeled for him. The other planned to create both hope and a new, tolerable reality, and he carried through on his plan. The same influences, circumstances, even genetic predispositions resulted in dramatically different effects or results. One man knew that he could commit himself to a plan and design his way out of anything. And he did. Sadly, the other, damaged twin did not.

In fact, recent psychological studies indicate that individuals who have suffered a severely dysfunctional childhood are just as likely to achieve greatness as they are to fail—due to precisely the same causal circumstances.

EXERCISE

Plan one work-related action and one random act of kindness for today. Note how you feel after you have completed them. Then formulate your PMS and PTP. Take them seriously, and work into them the vision and changing direction of a corporation or organization in which you are involved. Align your vision with that of your organization and note, within a week, the change in your attitude and performance. (If you are job-searching or determined to leave your current employer, write a personal mission statement and a personal tactical plan from scratch.)

In your PTP, make objectives (goals) and action steps for the short term, the intermediate term, and the long term—for approximately six months, two years, and five years. Remember to self-define and to describe your ideal life (in the present tense) and to attach pertinent steps toward its creation.

It is your design. Do not back away. Fight the fear (often disguised as skepticism) of making a commitment to yourself and to your life. Stick to your goals and plans of action. And do not give up if you hit a few detours. They are meant to come along to assist us in both the process and the arrival.

Plan. And renew your ability to dream.

Principle 11

Real Communication

Listen—always, not just when something meets your agenda. People and other parts of nature are trying to reach us. They need to be heard, and we need to hear them.

Strive to hear, understand, and acknowledge others first. Then, seek to be understood. The latter comes virtually automatically after the former.

Stephen Covey

Only partly because of the pace at which we lead our lives, we rarely stop to *really* listen to others. Just as problematic, we almost never stop to listen to our inner world, the sounds of nature, or the rhythmic sound of our own breathing, our life force. We are a society of vigilant self-activists, overtly and covertly self-preoccupied promoters and announcers, rather than sensitive receptors of others', messages and their marvels. As a consequence of this apparently necessary defensive posture, we are withering in expression, mutual connectedness, and personal performance.

These statements are not meant as condemnations. We were taught, early on, that "words are all we have" to earn the love, trust, and respect of others. In our early school years, we were rewarded for merely opening our mouths—10 points for participation—regardless of what we said. Ridiculously, this reality still exists in many work and social environments. The person who speaks most at meetings is often ascribed greater importance and power than those who wait until they have something relevant to say. Even if all the participants in a session have no idea what a speaker has been saying (and we usually think it is just we who don't understand the gobbledygook), they score points with wordy self-positioning. The old and tedious self-justifying trick of perorating for position—virtually the norm for years—is still acceptable input in stolid organizations.

Word Games

That we are a society fascinated by word games should not be surprising. Knowing more words than the next guy offers status. As a chronic reader of dictionaries, I am all for increasing the Grade 6 vocabulary of the average North American. However, words are used and abused in our lives to self-promote, seduce, and abuse, to proclaim and articulate empty love, to cheat, damage, and exclude. Words become, alternately, hugs and missiles. In that we place so much importance on what is said, rather than on observation and on really listening to what is conveyed, we are often injured, taken to the cleaners, or just plain humiliated by those who have made verbal presentation their major life tool. Words can be withheld, they can hound us, and they can back us into litigious corners, especially when used by individuals who have made *not* listening the other half of their modus operandi of control.

In short, words manipulatively spoken, blithely or deliberately, are just as dangerous as sticks and stones. As a therapist, I have seen more heartbreak, loss of self-esteem, self-disgust, even suicidal behavior result from the deliberately cruel or inadvertent misuse of words than from divorce, the death of loved ones, or any number of truly life-shaking tragedies. Unfortunately, words can leave unexcisable wounds in the depths of the human heart.

The manipulatively malevolent or innocently destructive use of words aside, we appear, perhaps understandably, to place much greater importance on the orifice beneath our noses than on those on either side of our heads. Most toddlers are hugged, celebrated, and lauded for days after they say their first words. And for most of us, that was just the beginning. The early educational system rewarded us more for talking and then, in our formative teenage years, we were told to shut up unless we said the right thing.

As adults, we appear to have vowed to regain the early acclaim and power that came with speaking to please. So many of us "blah, blah blahhed" our way through undergraduate degrees, imitating the style and articulating the ideas and opinions of the professors of the term. It was an easy art, and many of our self-deifying professors were easy marks. We even used the written word in bulk (quantity was at least as important as quality) to earn favor and an A-plus.

Today, in universities as in traditional workplaces, words and wordiness still triumph. *Communication,* in contrast, presupposes both two (or more) people and two fundamental facets: that one of those people has something pertinent and thoughtful to say to the other and that the other has been taken into consideration or has already been heard.

This simple situation rarely exists, however. When I teach "communication skills" to corporate employees, they are invariably surprised, even chagrined, over my spending a considerable amount of time on listening skills. Yet, by mere observation, we can see that the best communicators are attentive listeners. We see this skill (or lack of it) at work in social gatherings, on TV talk shows, and in workplace presentations. Those who do not listen rarely get the bang for their banter in the long run. Those who do listen are themselves heard and acquire the trust and respect of others. Consequently, they end up wielding considerable influence in and over their environment.

Listening, the Sensitive Sense

Listening is not only part and parcel of sound interpersonal communication. It is a sacred act and gift of recognition. In fact, listening is arguably the most important of the senses.

Too many of us either pay no notice to what is being spoken, breathily waiting for the other party to stop talking so that we can speak or jump in, merely repeating what we assume was said. Yet such replies psychologically nullify the person attempting to be heard. Because we were so celebrated in our early years for speaking, not to be responded to—or to be responded to with indifference or imitation—is to be left unheard. That is a heart-closer. We recede into ourselves and cease to contribute, regardless of the environment. And we cannot be fooled. We know when we are being heard and when we are not, as well as when the "hearer" is exerting no effort.

In brief, mouthing words that we know reach no one is humiliating. Yet it is common. Too many of us too often subject each other to this manipulative form of devaluation—without even knowing that we are doing it.

The life skill we have missed learning is the necessity of listening, even if only for self-serving reasons. Of course, most people claim that they *do* listen, hear, and know how to ask for input. But asking for input has become a tactical substitute for listening. In too many offices and boardrooms, notes are scribbled and heads nod but all in attendance have a tacit agreement that they will not hear anything that does not fit or is unexpected or unpleasant. Anyone who speaks the inordinate will be politely shut out.

Lack of listening is ubiquitous. We joke about passing neighbors asking how we are and reflexively responding with "good for you" after we say that we smashed our car on the way home from work yesterday and slept in a ditch waiting for help. And we laugh because these tales are true. We do not know how to take the time to listen. In fact, not listening is so much the ingrained norm that when someone does hear us and responds by asking more about what we said, we are either stunned or suspicious—and usually tongue-tied.

We are all too used to words being put in the air for no reason but to justify existence, to exert power, and to gain vantage. Particularly in the workplace, communication, in spite of all the ostensible attention given to it, is really about strategic noise-making. The wrong noises or words are withheld if they might be controversial. And if they are uttered by the brave or the naive, they are, in many organizations, still ignored or subsumed in the hubbub of comfortable, conventional chatter.

Yet new words and concepts should bring about change. Our commitment to communication and change is proportionate to our willingness to allow for the articulation of the hitherto ineffable—and to actually hear it. That is, we have to learn to actively listen to the mundane *and* to expressions of different, inordinate approaches or ideas in an environment protected by a pact of conformity.

Listening and Other Activities

Listening or not listening starts in the home. Countless times I have heard parents or spouses exclaim, after a tragedy or a divorce, "Why didn't I listen? I should have listened!" The epidemic of suicides among teenagers and young adults is, in large part, due to the fact that they do not feel connected to the ostensibly adult-controlled world. And one way to feel connected (valued) is to be heard attentively.

Being so busy, we too frequently listen to others as we do other tasks. Taking time to talk has come to mean taking time to join someone in an activity and talk on the side—like an order of dills with a sandwich. Listening has become a mere ancillary to the main course of doing. When we are otherwise engaged in something productive, we nod our heads and make affirming noises at the speaker precisely because we do not have to listen. Moreover, if the message is discomfiting, we can further submerge ourselves in the real task at hand. This is humoring the feelings of another, tantamount to just saying no to a request for attentiveness and care. True, valid, and connecting listening involves stopping other deflecting activities, being in stillness with the speaker, and being attentive to the facial, tonal, and other physiological dimensions of the message. Otherwise, we cannot receive the essence of the transmission.

The Greatest Gift

To the speaker, attentive listening feels, in a significant way, like profound acknowledgment and affirmation. Thus, the greatest gift we can give another human being is the sense that he is heard and understood. If those who are insecurely, manipulatively wordy only knew! Or, if they are lucky enough to have had children, if they could only remember the squirming excitement of a four-year-old when she has made herself clear. Big kids with mortgages and car payments are no different. The way to influence others is to ascertain and attend to what they think and feel, not to wow them with words. Used benevolently, the skill of active listening can create connections of immeasurable depth and value, both in the workplace and in the home, not to mention in traffic jams, in lineups, and, of course, in customer relations.

Listening is not merely to our circumstantial benefit. By being keener and more attentive to the full range of communication, we can also save ourselves needless pain and reap significant rewards. For example, when we announce we have fallen in love, we are, on one level, proclaiming both our emotional generosity and our desirability. By declaring our acumen for falling in love, we are saying much about ourselves and very little about the cause of our love. In our culture when we fall this way, we are, more often than not, caught up in blind obedience to our triggered needs and fanciful expectations. We actually, if unconsciously, precipitate our own fall of a different kind. Too frequently, we interpret who someone is by virtue of what he says. And we make these interpretations in accordance with our own needs, expectations, historic triggers, and blind spots. We then superimpose this highly charged image onto the object (or victim) of our love. Clearly, if we really listened, we would not fall so easily or, in some cases, so consistently, injuriously hard.

After the fall, we come to see what is real and what is not and to realize what some of the words of courtship might have signaled had we been sane at the time. We feel tricked, ripped off, or taken for a ride. Ironically, we use others to take ourselves for a ride precisely because we do not really listen to words spoken or to messages of the nonverbal kind. Deaf to anything but our own voice of experience and our own intertwined agendas, we have no one to blame but ourselves when our soulmate turns into Satan. Yet neither positive nor negative ascriptions can be fairly attached to someone in the historically driven heat of love-falling. So often, the other person had nothing whatsoever to do with the love-to-loss process. It is a matter of one or both parties having failed to listen. In effect, we are able to trick ourselves by fitting someone else's words and actions into a preconceived mold mentally manufactured to represent the perfect mate. And then, in time, our fantasy falls apart at the seams. Because of our fundamental emotional incompetence, we can go very quickly from love to hate.

Overall, the rewards that accrue from listening and hearing are immeasurable. They are, in total, the effortless glue that holds relationships and families together. They are also a multitude of positives in business, especially in areas such as sales and negotiation. A good listener and hearer adjusts her approach in accordance with the customer's valid needs, inner or expressed, and then readjusts according to what is communicated back. If a car salesperson thinks that what the customer wants is glitz when he is really concerned about service and reliability, the result will be no sale—or a bad one.

Regardless of what we do for a living, we underestimate the importance of hearing and acknowledging the expressed opinions, ideas, and needs, implicitly or explicitly expressed, of the people with whom we converse and work.

Listening and the New Workplace

As already mentioned, damaging miscommunication is almost par for the course in most places of work, even now when participation and inclusion are considered organizational priorities. Many quiet geniuses with innovative ideas have learned that they are not heard. Managers and supervisors (often empty talkers) assume that the quiet, uncharismatic employee has nothing to contribute and is of no political consequence. As a result, right from the beginning, quiet intelligence falls on deaf ears, and genius, wasted in resigned silence, remains unapplied.

Dynamic environments require working units in which every employee can expect to be heard. In such environments—and they do exist, if rarely—people exchange ideas and innovations as if they were comments on the weather. As a result, the participation rate in organizational or divisional shifts is extraordinary, and the level of commitment highly personal and intense. New endeavors are owned by all suggesters and listeners, and antediluvian, unworkable terms and artificial constructs such as *teamwork* are unnecessary. Given multiple inputs and a casual assumption of 100 percent buy-in, the attentive propulsion and productivity inherent in unity of purpose and contribution just happens.

This integrated momentum has to be preceded, however, by the consistent, experiential reality of acknowledgment, attentiveness, and respect. That is, each participant has to convey the need to hear what others have to say, accentuating the value of their opinions. That innovation and the mutually supportive sharing of knowledge are rare is perfectly understandable. Most of us do not like to appear to need to learn something from someone else. Soliciting the workings of brains other than our own requires both courage and humility. Yet that is the only way to legitimately seek, share, and elicit mutually supportive strengths and talents. To observe, ask, listen, and hear are skills and strengths. And ironically, they require revolutionizing the way we perceive our work and our personal and professional relationships.

We make an enormous mistake when we assume that someone has nothing to say. We are putting the onus on her, when the responsibility of conveying our interest is ours. The mere hint that someone's opinion does not matter closes down both the heart and the brain, the former just before the latter. An individual heart conveys acknowledgment, and then another heart responds, expanding or retreating in kind.

Listening and Leadership

The blithely uttered expression "managing from the heart" really means leading from a point of intense, democratic attentiveness. Indeed, perhaps the single most important leadership skill is active listening.

Although many people still refer by rote to *stress management, team building, project management,* and other buzz expressions that have failed (they were concepts that did not come to practical fruition because of the way they were conceived and taught), the notion of *active listening* seems to have gone by the wayside. It is seen as an inconsequential module in communication courses and it is virtually unmentioned in most corporate corridors and boardrooms. Perhaps the term has never been sufficiently trendy to package in corporate programs, philosophies, or mission statements. Or, perhaps subconsciously, decision makers deem it too yin to emphasize in the context of the yang of leadership.

Regardless of the reason, listening and mutual affirmation—the essence of coalescence, cooperation, shared mandates, and interpersonal commitment—are virtually omitted from today's managerial parlance. Yet they are at the core of rapport in leader-employee relationships. If a manager decides to become a leader, the first among the many people skills to really learn (not just espouse) is to listen and to ensure that speakers feel heard.

Managing by walking around, half of most successful leaders' schedules involves asking, listening, and ensuring that the speaker feels heard and acknowledged. This is precisely why they are the most successful leaders. The numbers related to productivity and profit prove it.

Indeed, the commitment, effort, and action required to listen, to encourage individual expression, and to ensure that others feel heard are fundamental components of all relationships and rapport. Listening, as part of real communication, is the antecedent both to valid, loving connections and to commercial success.

Listening, Beyond and Below the Din

Listening is a trust-inducing, resolving, and coalescing gesture of the most primitive human kind. Just as other species have ways in which trust is gained and lost and groups and hierarchies form, we as human animals have fundamental ways in which we convey safety and gain influence. Unfortunately, over the last 40 years, we have placed more emphasis on esoteric psychological matters than on fundamental anthropology and social science, losing sight of our animal nature. As human mammals, we have become so smart that we are incredibly dumb. Where interaction, love, and just being with each other are concerned, many of us are either inept or have lost touch. Some analysts argue that we have, on some level, deliberately absolved ourselves of essential, even easy intimacy in both our personal and professional relationships.

Creative production, friendship, partnership, and honest attentiveness require an authenticity of the most guileless and earnest kind. Paramount to this necessary intimacy is simple, kindly listening to the expressed opinions, ideas, feelings, and needs of others. In fact, as complex animals, we can connect at the level of heart by merely (but attentively) listening to words spoken.

Alternatively, we can maintain the uncaring, static-filled silence characteristic of benign noninvolvement by refusing to learn to do so. A conscious or unconscious refusal to listen to the utterances of another, either generally in day-to-day activities or episodically during a problem, is the equivalent of blithely dismissing a soul in the former case and of slapping the psyche of another in the latter. To simply listen and connect can eradicate seemingly immutable differences and change the course of the world, as was shown by two plain men, Mikhail Gorbachov and Ronald Reagan. It can also, in the increasingly competitive area of sales, of mutual funds or of lawn mowers, mean the difference between a win-win relationship and an ultimately contagious two-way loss.

Sham Listening

Too many of us today avoid our neighbors, ignore the subtleties of the messages from our children, pay only lip service to our partner, and fake sensitivity in our work. Some of us, particularly hitherto driven, successful men, cannot even have eye contact with a customer, especially a woman, let alone relate from the heart. Regardless of the particular situation, this approach to other human beings is a sham that is protective, even defensive, as we ourselves seek understanding, safety, and success in what increasingly feel like dangerous life environments. However, it leaves us in a very cold and dangerously unempathetic stalemate, both interpersonally and productively.

Even some managers of people businesses think that because employees can speak and even giggle spontaneously, they are communicating and building alliances. However, too many of these salespeople score with an initially connecting burst but cut the ostensible interest when they have a signature on a dotted line or a deposit in the bank. Indeed, even in firms related to public relations that did well in the personality-driven 1980s, really listening can be left out of the equation. I maintain a great distance from unthinkingly sloppy business outfits that dismiss soft souls, as well as potentially loyal clients, with a cute quip and a tight smile already affixed for the next paying customer.

In a whole new world in which what is real lasts and in which character, flawed but honest, is what counts, those who remain outside of the human heart, ignoring or uncaring, will last about as long as summer in the Yukon. More is demanded of us now than ostensible, expedient connections. Closed, competitive, and adversarial firms with happy faces on their letterhead are deaf to the signals from many places, including a highly sensitized and needy clientele. Market forces and the intimacy of once-distant geographic connections have created hypersensitive populations requiring, even demanding, that we communicate with clarity and integrity. It is business as unusual in a world that has little room for snazzy albeit deaf and dumb applications of prefab form over individualized substance. Inevitably, it is just good business practice to dump the bells and whistles and attend to real needs and messages from human hearts.

Natural Attachments

Amid the unhealthily boisterous nature of all our life environments, meaning is trying to reach us. Carl Jung calls the inner voice that speaks to us the voice of the *collective unconscious.* Non-Jungians refer to it as our *preconscious,* attempting to give us answers and guidance based on computations from stored memories and intuition. Still others say they have learned to listen to a *Holy Spirit,* or a *life spirit* representing holistic truths and inclusive goodness.

Regardless of what we call the source of messages related to stillness and natural connections, they are vital components of our actions and communication (if frequently ignored in our culture). Listening to what we may call the inner Self—the essential core of "us" through which this wisdom exists and flows—is a requisite for successful listening and living. The course of life cannot even be embarked on with any expectation of satisfaction without the inclusion of this sacred, guiding voice from within.

Yet only a highly successful minority of us humans—usually those who have learned the hard way not to ignore the messages that come in moments of stillness—have committed themselves to being attentive to this life-giving and lifesaving resource. For too many of us, the numbing din of our social and work environments still feels safer and more manageable (if more miserable) than the truths we might uncover in attentive silence and active connections.

No Lesser Sounds

Nature is also trying to speak to us, as are unconscious dimensions of ourSelves. The many messages inherent in the sounds of nature are part of our mammalian heritage and a necessary dimension of our life force. Getting away to a rural setting, a forest, or an ocean shore is not incidentally relaxing; it is primitively recharging. We *need* to hear the groaning sway of an aged tree, the varied sounds of birds, and the sweetly soothing cadence of gently, naturally running water. Like being rocked or held in the arms of a loving, securing mother, these natural sounds are physically and psychologically the closest that we can come to going home, to a feeling of natural safety.

Further and not coincidentally, the sounds of nature encourage and merge with the sounds of ourSelves. Increasingly, organizations are recognizing the importance of encouraging employees (and managers) to take the time to get and to stay in touch with a transcendent aspect of themselves—a dimension we share with all other living things.

In fact, in more and more places and spaces of frenetic, millennial activity, the word *spiritual* is being uttered more often and with reasonable if belated interest as a way to improve the lives, working conditions, and interrelationships of employees. Spirituality, long recognized and incorporated into the daily work life at organizations such as the World Bank, Boeing Corporation, and at least one division of RJR Nabisco, will not much longer be confined to whispered discussions by airy-fairy types in the mailroom. Indeed, *The Globe and Mail* ran an article on May 22, 1998, featuring a Royal Bank vice-president who feels that spirituality has to play a greater role in the lives of the necessarily productive. In most organizations, incentive programs and myriad corporate approaches toward employee evolution, cooperation, and motivation have proven expensive, demoralizing failures. Indeed, an article by Chris Argyris, professor of organizational behavior at Harvard University, posits a similar argument with respect to the efficacy of empowerment. In the *Harvard Business Review* of May/June 1998—he stresses the importance of "internal involvement" over "external programmatic incentives." The latter, he points out, change little if any of an employee's (or a manager's) perspective toward his or her work or organization. "Programs" per se fail without the potency of individual "internal involvement."

Without attuning ourselves, in quietude, to whispers from shared spaces and beginnings, we work in rote allegiance to external rule. Without intangible connections and beliefs, we too often, especially now, "strut and fret" knowing or feeling that our work is "signifying nothing" or, at best, very little. Some individuals in hierarchically higher places are beginning to see and even dare to speak of the necessity of beliefs beyond the buck. It takes little imagination to understand that allowing for the expression, inclusion, and respect for connections of all kinds is empowering, motivating, and directing amid the velocity and volume of seemingly valueless modern human requirements. We have known and denied for centuries that unifying and steadying connections among our Selves and all life forms, along with a sense of purpose and a personal design for a life, can guide us with unworldly certitude.

We are way beyond needing to smell the roses. We need to lie still in nature—on a woodsy knoll, by the ocean, or on a sun-drenched crag, to reexperience the wise unity of living rhythms. Much can be heard, clarified, and healed in living sounds and in silence. Ironically, however, most of us relegate nature to accidental or planned moments during vacations from the imprisoning unreality of real life. And our sense of something greater than ourselves is too often a mere flicker of a thought as we click the television past the Discovery channel.

The Myriad Messages

We get back to ourselves by listening, which involves making internal connections with ourSelves and others. We also get back to ourSelves by accepting and reuniting with our ineradicable connection to everything and everyone around us, including those we merely brush by on the street, those who annoy us, and those whose behavior indicates that they are in trouble or lost. If we listen, all things will speak to us, and all messages, words, and natural sounds can provide us with insight. Even working in a garden is, to some, an enlightening, even spiritual experience. Many claim to be renewed by the process and openly admit to having been given something through or by their experience with seeds and earth. Whether our path involves being alone and still for a moment on a ski trail or quietly observing and listening beyond the words in a boardroom, we have to commit ourselves to listening in order to hear, learn, and grow in whatever form is appropriate or pertinent to our lives. We are deaf to much—including our own breathing and the unbridled laughter of children still unafraid—that would both lighten the load and light us with joy.

Finally, listening and hearing in relation to the other principles of this book is critical. We cannot reduce fear, forgive, change our thinking, or plan our lives without listening to the naturally mysterious and solitudinously silent directives that are omnipresent to assist us. Individuals who are acculturatedly deaf to the subtleties of life cannot make contributions, nor can they, sadly for us all, find and manifest their unique dimensions of genius and greatness.

Listening is a life skill worth learning—even late. The rewards and the kinds and degrees of enrichment are infinite, as are the messages, human and otherwise, awaiting our attention. To advertently or inadvertently tune out is to be deaf to all human possibility, from love to successful employment. What we cannot hear, we cannot see as either opportunities for positive influence or as sane sources of support and contribution.

CASE STUDY

John and Myra Learn the Need for Expressed Attentiveness

In my diagnostic work with employees, their most common complaint is that their opinions do not matter. When I speak to their managers, however, most want to hear more, not less from employees.

I hear exactly the same complaints about communication in most marriages. Usually the wife explodes with anger after many years, during which she has felt and claims that her husband does not listen. Yet I have heard husbands recite everything their wives have said in the last 10 years.

A case in point were a couple, Myra and John. After 15 years of marriage, Myra felt that John ignored everything she said, and she insisted that he accompany her to a counselor. Unless he became more attentive, she told him in no uncertain terms, their marriage was over.

By the end of their second session, it was clear that John was a quiet man by nature, that Myra was very talkative, and that their conversations at home were one-sided. However, it also became clear that John *did* hear virtually every word his wife uttered. In fact, Myra was astounded when, in the middle of a session, John referred to and expanded on a variety of her complaints from over the years. She had no idea that he had listened to her, let alone computed the information.

In simple fact, all John needed to do was to learn how to show that he was listening: with body language, with eye contact, and with the odd word to confirm his attentiveness. Soon he felt less confused and hurt by what had been his wife's claim that he wasn't listening—her major, daily complaint for years. He had done nothing wrong; he simply needed to do a few more things right to ensure that Myra *felt* heard and acknowledged.

So common as to be commonplace, a real problem with listening as part of successful communication is the lack of both active (obvious) listening and some form of communication that conveys to the other individual that she or he is being heard and that the expressed opinion, suggestion, or need is being attended to. The male half of one couple I counseled swore up and down that he "damn well listened" as his wife "went on and on" and that she was just looking for problems. Particularly between the sexes, distinct, concrete signals are needed to indicate the intake and processing of expressed information. As humans, we do not feel heard unless it is virtually proven to us in the form of gestures or pertinent responses.

Indeed, in all the case studies I could bring to this principle, the importance of listening and understanding first applies. Ensure that the other people in your life feel heard, and then put in your own two cents. It is merely human nature—but it works like magic.

EXERCISE

Daily, listen and deliberately hear beyond the words of at least two people. Do this until it becomes automatic with everyone in your life. Note the difference in the way you are perceived and received, as well as how you start to feel about others.

Also daily, find a way to be in contact with a part of nature: an animal, a tree, even your lawn (or someone else's). Observe and sense it. Feel yourself freed, with no fears, no agendas, and no musts as you respond to what exists, growing and living before you. Soon you will be able to—and should—note the renewed or released flow of wisdom from many places, spaces, and faces. It will be increasingly difficult to be anything but attentive and curious in all your life endeavors.

Principle 12

Giving and Receiving

Know that giving and receiving are the same. That is the real win-win technique.

We have learned, in a society based on exchange, competition, and an absence of trust, to give only when there is the promise of an equal or greater reward. Yet it is only unconditional giving that truly alights hearts and carries with it the promise of a return.

John Murphy

If I can show them how I feel, that I don't know everything, that I need them and learn from them, that we really are a team, we can do anything.

Stephen G. Zanarini, vice-president, IBM Global Services, a legend in all but his own mind

I know a handful of truly generous people. For the most part, they are individuals or couples who no longer have to prove themselves in and to the world. They have attained financial security, if not great wealth, and they simply and unconditionally enjoy sharing with others. They give, materially and otherwise, in a matter-of-fact manner and, most significantly, without the strain of presumed reciprocity. Further, they give for truly selfish reasons. They share because doing so makes them feel good, closer to others, and in a small but cumulative way, as if they can make a positive difference in the lives of others. They would assert that they benefit much more than those to whom they give.

Fearful Paucity

As already mentioned in a variety of ways, we have been taught to be grippers rather than givers, to horde rather than to give away something that we no longer need, and to withhold those intangibles that seem to be in finite supply. It started when we were toddlers and clued in to the apparent power of ownership; it culminated in adulthood as signified by phrases such as "I gave at the office." The majority of us still think that locking our doors, constantly looking over our shoulders, and keeping an eye on our wallets and other possessions is the way to secure what we perceive as our limited abundance.

Within reason, we do have to secure our belongings. However, *hypervigilant* protection of our things indicates an intense, preoccupying, and imprisoning sense of paucity. It is also invariably linked to the suspicion that other people—all other people—are in some way intent upon ripping us off.

Unfortunately, those of us in North American culture who are not among the superrich have a sense of paucity—a fearful and possessive belief in scarcity and limitation. It affects and restricts both our will and our ability to be generous. We are even loathe to give away our emotions, to share our feelings, or to offer goodwill. Many potentially complex psychological issues aside, it is as if we think that we have a finite supply of "us-ness," kindness, and love.

A case in point: I recently heard an apparently effective manager sneer at an employee's expressed disappointment in her superior's officious behavior. The manager said, "Listen, toots, I save my sweetness for home!" Ironically, her husband gets the same line but with respect to her managing people at the office.

For when and for whom are we reserving our tenderness, our kindness, even our tears? Have we not yet learned the value of being randomly, easily, effortlessly kind, even if only in the sense of understanding that what goes around comes around?

Price-Tag Giving

The giving and getting of tangible, material things, especially our blushing, barely self-controlled reception of cash, is what we know and compute best. Even though we can never really win at this game, we evaluate our worth, measured against the gift, and calculate reciprocity. How many of us have mangled our brains trying to think of an equivalently valuable gift—at least one that might seem to be as valuable to a hopefully naive giver? The most obvious annual gift-giving contest is, of course, Christmas. For most of us, it is invariably a material debacle of the hair-pulling, no-win kind. A prize should go to the "Christmas champion" who has figured out how to play this game well, unlike the rest of us who please the fewest possible number of people the greatest possible number of times—in spite of our level of postholiday indebtedness.

This "Christian" exemplar of self-aggrandizing excess and upmanship has become the surest way to set ourselves up for a series of self-eroding experiences with exacerbated inadequacy and guilt. How many of us have lost sleep over having failed to correctly calculate the value of an expected gift and ended up under giving in return? It is a mortifying moment when the lesser gift is opened by a tightly smiling associate or friend-become-potential-opponent, who, we know, will now not speak to us for a year. At the end of that time, by tacit understanding, we will have a chance to redeem ourselves by providing a gift of at least quadruple value, while the gift we receive (if any) will be distinctly cheap. We commit and resign ourselves to this strategic balancing act as punishment, vindication, and symbolic reparation of the valued relationship.

Such "giving" is actually barter, and it even makes liars out of us. How many of us have received a gift, smiled pleasantly while saying that we have left the giver's gift upstairs, and then, leaving him slightly perturbed and suspicious, sprinted to frantically search for what I call a *chain gift*? We all have some—gifts previously received and stockpiled in sundry places in our homes because we cannot bear to exhibit them or to throw them out. Inevitably, we sacrifice them to the ritualistic barter. We get good at it (praying that no object works its way back to the original giver), and we loathe ourselves and the recipients for being players in the tricky, dishonest process. And on it goes. The season ends, a few children get a gift high for approximately two hours, and we wish we had done church.

In these situations and others, we are competitive givers. We give bitterly from a position of real, strained limitation, as well as from a place of imagined, inner paucity. We give when we have to, and when we do, we calculate and manipulate to ensure appearances and to procure favor. It is human social politics. We are too angry to give of ourselves, too pent up to dare to feel or to show too much feeling (we might weep and never stop). Genuine emotion is deemed unworkably awkward and dangerous.

Material giving is a cover-up. We give gifts to express something in order to get gifts that mean something. No one dares to give the assiduously, systemically guarded gift of feelings or the clarity of commitment. After all, "What if everyone decided to get all emotional?" as one middle-aged bank executive recently asked his daughter. The strained theater of daily life might come tumbling down, making us real and leaving us with just Selves and Others in need of something "real-ly" given.

Giving and Getting

Material giving is entirely out of control, out of context, and ritualistic. It is another must in schedules during which we often run on emotional empty. And, needless to say, few people give just to give. In fact, when someone does give unconditionally, he is often faced with some suspicion or at least a pensive query about the motivation behind the act.

Given this cycle, many of the minority of human beings who really do want to give unconditionally ultimately stop, finding the act of generosity more complex or problematic than it is worth.

Giving for the mere sake of giving should be simple, easy, and matter-of-fact. It is not, however, on our this-is-mine and that-is-yours material treadmill. If no quid pro quo is immediately discernible, we make one up with our rabidly suspicious imaginations and wait, a mental hand on our hip, to be hit up for our part of the exchange. We find it virtually impossible not to question the giver, thus missing the act of unconditional generosity.

We can wait in that judgmental position forever. True givers want only the gift of unfettered giving. They do not involve themselves in the bartering process that defines and drives our make-as-much-as-you-can-but-remain-tight-fisted games and gains. Given our inane approach to each other, what we get and give is often another deflecting, symbolic measure of our worth and the worth of others. And more frequently than any of us will admit, the exchange is empty of meaning and touches no one.

Strange Giving

Recently, a delightful man held a door for me (all men who hold doors for women, men, children, or chimps with their arms loaded with bags are delightful). Some women, myself included, do the same for anyone who happens to reach the door at the same time. And some of us automatically reach out a hand to help a parent struggling with a stroller on stairs or a fellow pedestrian with a balky bundle buggy. What astounds me is the number of people who miss this and other small opportunities to positively affect a moment, hour, or day in the otherwise harried, often empty and arduous life of another human being.

Letting other drivers into traffic can be the same kind of small-enormous gift. Most people who do not give it are not selfish, self-centered boors. They are merely lost in thought and deaf and blind to the presence and needs of others. Further, they don't think of others as needing virtually the same thing they need. And sadly, they have forgotten how good it feels to help someone by simply stopping one car length sooner before a red light.

We have come to seek our gratification in more difficult and complex ways. Now more than ever, we attempt to self-gratify by reaching for—and never acquiring—perfection or security at work or by scoring points for appearing to have a faint idea of what we are doing with respect to the latest corporate vision. It's easier to just hit the brakes.

Anger and Rescinding

I know too many otherwise terrific people who proudly declare that they no longer hold doors or let others into traffic. When asked why, they indignantly exclaim that they never receive ample if any gratitude for their efforts. Bingo! What they are looking for is barter.

In virtually all circumstances, when we give, we expect something in return, even if it is just recognition that we are wonderfully generous, and considerate individuals. But giving cannot work this way. Frequently, a driver who has received a break acts as if the traffic magically parted for her, and someone who has had a door held for him behaves as if it automatically swung open when it sensed his presence. In brief, there is often no recognition whatsoever of an act of thoughtfulness or kindness. *And this has to be okay.*

Giving, if real, is "no expectations giving." Waiting for a response or a reward for our kindness virtually negates the act of giving. So what if it elicits no grateful response? The giving still feels both right and necessary—especially for those of us who understand the distinctly personal, human struggle hidden behind the tight visages of the apparently uncaring.

Regardless of whether or not people show any recognition of having been helped, they are unquestionably and positively affected, even if only subconsciously. Being assisted computes during the seconds, minutes, and days of the lives of both giver and receiver. Therefore, as much as is humanly possible, we should be sanguine about the preoccupied blindness of others—and about the pervasive, impersonal presumption of competition and insensitivity. We play games with each other in strange ways, especially as strangers. We say and do things (in traffic, for example) that we would be embarrassed if our children heard or witnessed. Through their eyes we would see that we too are frantically grabbing and vying for vantage. We would also appear to be mundanely at war with each other, rather than in any way connected by mutual consideration. Our children would certainly not be able to see beyond the apparent contempt to the fact that we are suffering and needing in identically simple ways.

Small Things, Big Gifts

Unrequited giving—to colleagues, friends, family members, or strangers—is an oxymoron. It is also an embittering, market-driven perceptual construct in the mind of the non-giver. Yet many of us, if not most, believe in this concept. We are well trained in vigilant, moment-to-moment, multidimensional, and directional competition. We are so overcome by holding on, gripping, with a sense of having so little left yet so much to lose that if we merely smile at someone and receive no smile in return, we are hurt and indignant and then even contemptuous of the privileged recipient of our gesture. Unconsciously, we feel that the conditions of our warmth have not been met, so we have wasted our kindness.

Perhaps understandably, we are keeping increasing tabs on what little we are giving to each other in the way of assistance and basic kindness. Because of our recently increasing feelings of disconnectedness, inadequacy, and insecurity, we are taking fewer and fewer risks toward creating meaningful connections. We are becoming stockkeepers, conscious of our rapidly depleting emotional inventories. Urgently and unequivocally, we need a theologian, a social scientist, a medical practitioner, or a management consultant to help us shift our perceptions and risk giving for the sake of our knotted hearts, as well as in the name of true quality of life.

Small, helpful acts of support and kindness are usually all that we have to give to strangers. Of the few ways we can show love for them, most have no built-in payback. The implicit gift of giving—the inherent reward, if there has to be one—is merely that we have a chance to give, that no matter how we feel, we always have something of value to share with or give away to another heart. The reward is in knowing that we ourselves have value precisely because we can bring something positive to the lives of others.

Unconditional giving frames our worthiness. It is the way we can add value to our own lives, as well as those of others, regardless of our mood or circumstances. Creative giving in a seemingly ungiving world is fundamental to our mental health. It nurtures us, keeps us healthy and strong, and allows others to benefit from not-too-distant care if they happen to stop, listen, feel, and enjoy.

Job Sharing and Leadership

A tremendous irony is at work in our lives. Studies show that a majority of us hesitate to get up in the morning, let alone to haul ourselves to what many perceive as the office from hell where we work with our colleagues from hell and answer to clients from hell under the supervision of a boss from hell. Friday evening is reserved either for collapsing or for partying until we have to be sent home in a taxi. On Saturday, we recover, and on Sunday, the tension builds and the weekly headache kicks in as we ready ourselves for our work life.

Thus, we say we hate going to work. *Hate* is a frightfully and frighteningly strong word, but it describes the way in which too many of us function within our income-producing environments.

One of the reasons the experience is so dreadful is that many of us feel we have nothing to give to that environment or to the people who populate it. Nor, in many cases, do we feel like contributing anything. The chaotic nature of the times is such that we feel insecure, angry, and defensive, and we have vowed, consciously or unconsciously, to give no more than we perceive ourselves as getting. Thus, we give very little, if anything, of ourselves to the job or to the people around us—and vice versa.

Except in firms blessed with powerful, enlightened, and courageous leadership, the barter approach has burgeoned and pervaded ever-changing, unpredictable, and self-driven workplaces. And uncomprehending employees experience these environments as unappreciative, punitive, and ruthless. Forget about chitchat and courses on teamwork, cooperation, and sharing knowledge—what's the payback?

A critical support for employees experiencing the strain of change or the millennial malaise and maze involves leadership that, by definition, ensures the presence of built-in incentives, tangible and emotional, to become involved, speak out, share, take risks, and work and play from the heart. The new leader is unafraid of her own emotions, especially unbridled enthusiasm and an expressed love of people, and thereby manages from the heart in order to get a heartful return from employees. She knows that giving—by risking the expression of positive, rewarding, verbal generosity or by tangible gifts, via profit-sharing or sporadic, surprise bonuses—begets giving.

Emotionally generous management and employee units have profoundly better bottom lines, whether measured by office morale, low levels of absenteeism, or significantly higher profits. Even amid uncertainty, with no guarantees regarding the future, giving to, caring for, or rewarding involvement communicates worthiness and value. And if we human beings feel that we are valuable, we feel, ipso facto, that we have something worth giving and have a natural will to do so.

Thus, the new leader-management principle of employee cooperation and productivity is that giving and receiving are the same. Once the cycle has started and been tended to without vigilant expectation, there evolves a natural momentum based on multiple wins and a natural, reflexive ease of coalescent productivity and performance.

You First

Most of us prefer to have others make a trail before we follow. We do the same thing with the expression of our emotions. But in our work and in our overlapping private lives, we cannot accept the habitual norm and wait to be given to before we risk giving. This is a no-win situation, emotionally positioned for mutual or multiple disappointments.

At one time or another, we have all been inspired to give and we have done so. But the first time that our gesture went unacknowledged, we recoiled and again withheld—waiting for someone else to give first. The waiting has to stop.

In order to give unconditionally, we have to analyze and come to understand our emotionality as it relates to our reluctance or inclination. Giving-to-get giving is more of the false perceptual construct that too many of us have been trying to make workable. The tried and true fact remains: we earn more loyalty, love, and, indeed, unconditional generosity from others by giving with no strings attached. Our gifts may elicit no immediate, clear response but in the not so long term, there will be both trust and a will to reciprocate. More than likely, the initial answer will have nothing to do with payback but rather be an awkward, tentative gesture from a nascently credulous heart.

As humans, we have to express our need to give and to make giving habitual. Giving inspires others to behavior, actions, and tasks that cannot be induced by a well-written code of conduct, a morale-building session, or admonishments about increased cooperation and generosity. The act of giving itself speaks loudly to hungry, frightened hearts, whether the generosity is displayed by a colleague or a sibling. This essential, basic truth is taking the place of old tricks and strategies included in the curricula of MBA programs a mere three or four years ago. We had become so smart and so determined to find fancier, high-tech ways and strategic messages to use to induce behavior in those around us that we lost touch with what works with functioning minds and easily delighted hearts. Who would, in this day and age, truly believe that what really works from a management perspective is homegrown, unconditional generosity and basic kindness?

The same approach is also foundational to today's family counseling strategies. Substance over style has always been the way to honestly motivate the human heart.

We really do have to give just for living's sake. We have to be free to give, materially and mentally, without expectations in order to create together and to be together in productive or loving endeavors. Repeatedly giving what is free or unconditional inspires the currently rare inner posture of trust. And it is when we trust that we feel trusted, respected, and valued. It is also then that we stop distinguishing between giving and receiving and just do for and in synchronicity with each other.

CASE STUDY

Jack and Sam Get and Give

One of Jack Welch's key winning characteristics is his reflexive generosity with employees and managers. Guru and chief executive officer of General Electric until recently, he gave and trusted first and dealt with problem people once they came to light. He was emotionally generous, as well as renowned for handing out spot bonuses from his own pocket. And his giving, caring posture toward all his employees obviated any need to impose standards, punch cards, or other forms of employee monitoring.

Welch has since been snatched from General Electric by another multinational corporation, where he is instituting the same culture, and, as expected his giving is already resulting in gains to the bottom line.

Similarly, Sam Walton of WalMart still holds a generous avuncular place in his people's hearts despite the growth of his business.

Interestingly, Walton and his senior management had a much more difficult time reaching the hearts of Canadians when the firm reached north from the United States. Potential Canadian employees were distinctly distrustful, even openly cynical, about both the man and the approach. *The Globe and Mail* quoted Walton as saying, jokingly, "Don't you people believe in or get excited about anything up here?"

The question was asked in jest after a failed first rally outside of Toronto in 1995. Now, of course, Walmart is marking stores such as Zellers and K-Mart for a quick death unless they breathe some life into their cultures. Even in Canada, Walmart employees feel given to, valued, cared for, and trusted.

Although Walton's gratitude and generosity to all his employees—often in the form of hugs and kisses—may never sweep the Canadian landscape, he has applied the simple principle of giving in order to get. His employees consistently aim to please; they work in anticipation of expressed appreciation, and the seemingly unsophisticated system has built-in rewards to ensure that they get their due. The jokes from nervous Canadian business pundits are decreasing, and the unpolished yet brilliantly contrived and sustained culture continues to make everyday a heyday. This international win-win style is fascinatingly simple.

EXERCISE

Each day, do something for someone, even a stranger, and keep it to yourself. Anonymous giving is the most memorable and genuine kind.

BY WAY OF SANITY

Also daily, go one step further to assist someone at work with some information or a tip. As a manager-become-leader—someone who inspires others to work for the heart—give of yourself (including your foibles) and share your enthusiasm. Disregard virtual contractual agreements related to exchange, and inspire others with your sense of abundance and your singular generosity of spirit. It will be modeled and effortlessly returned in kind.

Principle 13

Self-Management

Know what you are thinking, and think what you know. Do not entertain fearful thinking, speculation, or suspicion without doing an immediate reality check. Your thoughts rule and create your life.

I would not want to be here, to try to contribute here, if I could not manage my inner world so as to best allow for the expression of my strengths, my talents and my love.

Ralph Waldo Emerson

Whether you think you can or you think you can't, you are absolutely right.

Henry Ford

In a book about the fundamentals of sane and successful living in the new millennium, the principle of managing how, why, and what we think and believe is not just the cherry topping a sundae. Rather, it is the essence of nourishment per se.

What we think, when and how intensely we think, what beliefs our thinking sustains, and even what we think about our thinking are key components of the cognitive composite that defines and directs us. Cognitive organisms, directed by interrelated logic and emotion, we have conscious and unconscious thoughts, as well as energy related to them, and they align or disalign us with reality. What we think and believe is who we are and how we perform with or against new realities.

Recall, from the Introduction, my explanation of why the principles in this book total 13, a number that has, for centuries, held many captive in a superstitious, unempirical belief that it is unlucky or lucky. True to human form, the vast majority of us in western cultures have chosen the negative over the positive (just in case!) and fear over hope.

Our superstitious reaction to a mere numeral is a simple example of the fact that we are really elementary thinkers—silly smartypants who pay little attention to what motivates and drives us. In fact, most of us do not even know what we really think about anything, let alone how to use our thinking, our mental steering mechanisms, to manage our increasingly complex lives.

Rethinking

We have much to rethink, including the choices we make around meaning and method in our daily lives. Our cognitive repertoires include too many false beliefs. Only through an examination and revision of our core beliefs can we set ourselves free to be who we are—or can be. To be bound either by the antiquated beliefs of a torpid culture or by personal historic beliefs with no current relevance to our lives is to disable ourselves in the face of new, uniquely human challenges.

Indeed, much of North Americans' present trouble and struggle is due to our holding on to the beliefs and axioms of another age. Culturally, we remain mired in definitions and directives from circa 1950, although structurally, socially, and economically we have leapt into an entirely new period and experience in human history. Our belief systems—our directing, cognitive footholds—are irrelevant, even dangerous. In hunkering down in an epidemic of defensive mental and emotional postures, we are in group denial of the social revolution of which we are a part; we are also further disabling ourselves for participation in it.

Denial makes for dormancy, and we are seeing this destructive inertia in well-meaning employee and community populations in every corner of the western world. Ironically, as events and daily responsibilities have multiplied and accelerated, many of us have slowed to a stunned stop. Old beliefs and wrong thinking have us stymied from within and feeling frightened and inadequate from without. And most of us fear using the key to self-renewal and full participation in a world a half a century beyond our thinking.

Reexamining Perceptual Constructs

In having to adjust to dramatic changes in the workplace, face the increasing prospect of working independently of organizations, or cope with changing personal relationships, we all have reason for self-challenging mental deliberations.

Yet most people are at a loss as to how to change in accord with new mandates, organizational or social. In-depth, intrapsychic change does not come naturally to the human animal, especially under the kinds of pressures that make us reflexively cling to old spaces and places in thought and emotional resistance. To rethink our thinking is more unnatural to most of us than is switching which hand we write with. However, there is no other way to change our thinking and limit our reactivity so as to make the former more pertinent and useful to new realities. Nor is there a better way to acquire the acuity, agility, and flexibility required for current endeavors. We are stunted if we are thinking the old way—in left-brain, linear, rote, repetitive obedience to an antiquated model of work and success. Even if we feel ripped off by sudden changes in the rules, we have to learn them, flow with them, and apply them. Neither can we forever abide by the new rules. They too will change and keep changing.

Thus, we have to make inner, cognitive adjustments in order to stay with the ever-changing, rapidly developing nature of organizational mandates, work styles, and lifestyles. If we do not, we are the equivalent of once-valuable racehorses, now handicapped and resigned to an illusory pasture from the past. As human beings, our handicap is our inability to reevaluate, replace, and remain vigilant about the thinking that lies at the foundation of our beliefs, our perceptions, our attitudes, our focus, and our decisions and actions. Only the process of reevaluation and resultant "response-ability" can free us from long-conditioned reactivity and allow for the decoding and self-reprogramming of the way of the day.

Our current perceptual constructs are neurological and cognitive programs that continue to kick in regardless of the changing nature of our responsibilities. They automatically take over and have us approach new challenges with old mental software, as well as antiquated expectations and consequential disappointments and frustrations. Yet we cling to them like twigs on a cliff, to the detriment of our mental and physical health, rather than finding the courage to secure our footing and climb back up against gravity. Barring a near-death experience or life-shaking trauma, we are inveterately lazy thinkers, unlikely to find sufficient purpose to challenge the ostensible, historic security of our inner worlds. Our beliefs and habitual cognitive postures once served us well. As a result, we are reluctant to dismiss them merely because of social and organizational change. Many of us still think that a return to normality is just around the corner. In fact, *normality* has long been absent from the vocabulary of modern living.

Continuous Learning

Continuous learning, one of the more familiar buzz phrases of the past decade, is a farce in most of today's organizations. Like self-managed, self-directed thinking, continuous learning should, by virtue of mere common sense, have been inculcated in us in grade school.

The *learning organization* (also popular cant) is virtually an oxymoron. In my work with hundreds of organizations, I have been involved with only a few that actually understand the concept, actively encouraged and supported it, and viewed continuous learning and individual growth as being equally as important as operational imperatives. So, not surprisingly, the vast majority of employees view both organizational change and the notion of self-change as a personal threat, thereby invoking an emotional and cognitive mindset antithetical to growth and participation, let alone to continuous, ongoing learning.

Although many organizations pay lip service to the notion that people are the greatest asset, most ignore the next active step. Moreover, few of those who steer the human organisms and the programs established to encourage growth and change have the faintest idea how individual employees are to meet the mandate.

For the most part, experience and studies show, employees do not change because they have no idea what is being asked of them in the way of visceral transformation. Few organizations and senior managers dare to address the how of employee repositioning. As a result, most employees continue to wing it with a renewed sense of insecurity and inadequacy, assuming that they are not getting something others have figured out. They continue to work the old way and hope that no one notices.

Thus, the mandate of the learning organization has come to mean nothing other than "catch up and stay with us if you can." The concept of continuous learning directly conflicts with other, culturally prevailing views, especially the notion that life comprises learning years, during which we go to school; earning years, during which we stay in one place, collecting a paycheck and pension qualifications; and yearning years, when we retire and wish we were still earning income by showing up somewhere five days a week. In spite of frequent and popular discussions to the contrary, this sequence is still considered the natural order of things. Indeed, much of the North American working population still tightly grips this false belief, with its underlying sense of security.

We should, of course, perceive continuous learning, growing, and exploring personal and human possibilities as the natural course of human development—and, incidentally, as fundamental to employability or personal market value. Yet neither explanation nor incentive has ever been fully or clearly articulated to the average individual. Nor, even now that we know the destruction wreaked by closed minds and finite learning, are our organizations and institutions teaching the fundamental how-to of ongoing learning, individual adjustment, and personal responsibility. The fallout from this gap in our education toward and in adulthood is both enormous and tragic—not to mention horrendously expensive.

Mental Self-Management and Relationships

We exhibit the same resistance to using our heads in order to adjust and improve our personal and professional relationships. When partners or associates change or grow, a crisis is likely to ensue because of our inability to fathom and actuate self-change. (In fact, a cardinal rule among those who have achieved is to keep plans and goals a secret; otherwise, the fearful resistance of others will present success-breaking obstacles.) We fear change, especially positive attitudinal change among those close to us personally or at work. It threatens us because we experience it unconsciously as a reflection of our own inertia and confusion. We also fear being left behind.

Indeed, those among us who choose self-change and self-management are extremely rare. Without training, only a tiny fraction of any adult population naturally adjusts and grows with unwanted external change. In fact, most of us deem the notion of self-change so mammoth and improbable that we treat it as a problem of pathological dimensions. For example, people seek marriage counseling, more often than not, because one member of the relationship has changed, while the other has not or will not.

The need for change is seen as a major, arguably insurmountable problem precisely because we, as human thinkers, have not learned to use our heads to adjust, even in minor ways, without major incentives. Indeed, this fundamentally prosaic challenge is perceived as a negative, an assault on a completed self, and a major threat to our inner worlds. Although the adage that "when we stop learning and growing, we are dead" has become a platitude, we as individuals and as organizations composed of individuals ignore it, accepting as par the lack of growth and unmanaged thoughtlessness of the living dead.

Reconsidering Mental Stasis

The quality of our human rapport in organizations and in partnerships says much about the quality of our work and the longevity of our marriages. Sound, honest, and creative rapport between and among human beings is implicitly defined by growth and change, by latitude for individuality, and by circumstantial adjustment. No other genre of positive rapport exists. Yet many of us maintain associations, even ostensibly profound connections, based on mutual, tacitly agreed-upon stasis.

Moreover, many of us who might otherwise attempt to change or grow in our personal or work relationships, choose not to so as to avoid offending others. Most of us want to float on perpetually still waters and watch movement from afar. No one taught us to ride the wave of change or to celebrate what is often a healthy (if unavoidable) incentive to take on the next major crest of personal connections. The intransigence hurts us as partners, as parents, and with other people in general. It also, needless to say, impedes us in the workplace. In spite of our apparent intelligence, many of us are stuck-in-the-mud dumb. We want and need to be valued and loved—without having to manage adjustments in our perspectives, attitudes, and actions.

By nature and by nurture, we fear change and will do anything we deem effective to stop it or stall it—including attempting to stunt the growth of others. Poor behavior it is, but it is all most of us know. A bird in the hand? Grip it and grip it some more, even if we have to crush it to keep it with us and to keep it the same.

In contrast, self-managed people can let go. They see change coming and make mental and emotional adjustments accordingly. They view change as both a challenge and an opportunity.

Back to the Future

With more than 70 percent of the working population claiming to hate what they do for income and with more than two out of three marriages disintegrating amid modern chaos, new ways of thinking, being, and doing are in order. Ironically, while battles rage over how to increase technological competency among high school graduates, we have yet to establish a mean level of mental and practical competency in the fundamental areas of thinking and adaptability. Our technologies have moved beyond us, creating more and more demanding work than we are able to process.

Yet unless we learn how to work more productively by making changes in our perspective, newer and faster technology will merely ensure that we become even less adept in our efforts. Instead of creating leisure time, as once predicted, our technology has created "seizure time"—days spent in spasmodic tension and fear as we run to catch up and never do. The average person, well educated and successful as recently as the mid-1980s, now faces a whole new, personally challenging (and debilitating) world. With no concrete rules or strategies for success, many of the once willing and devoted are stunned in their tracks by both confusion and anger. Mental acuity and agility, never positioned as requisites for successful living, are now critical to success and sanity. Yet we have never felt so stupid or so stunned in the face of the inescapable need for growth.

Moreover, the how of increased mental and emotional agility is absent from organizational and social parlance. "Just do it" makes people hunker down in fear states replete with unresourceful past programming and angry resistance. So does "just learn it." The desperate human brain goes into neurological download at the mere hint of unknown, unexplained contingencies.

We have to let our thinking processes go back before they can legitimately go ahead.

Cognitive Reprogramming

What no one is fully explaining to floundering and frenzied employee populations is that what we learned and how we learned it is no longer pertinent to new and changing realities. For example, to horde knowledge in order to have power over others no longer works in our favor. We cannot even decipher which knowledge to horde. Moreover, to memorize and imitate, until recently the keys to successful academic endeavors as well as to promotability in most organizations, are now virtually useless methods of performance and manipulation. We were never taught to learn, only to strategize, to adopt technique, and to mimic the style of the moment.

In the workplace, our efforts and perceptual acuity were devoted to a kind of strategic seduction. In personal relationships, we were taught to barter in different but just as inauthentic, self-protecting, and self-limiting ways. All our successful rapports were those we cultivated so as to gain favor with important or significant others.

In fact, our current agenda, fully understood, is not as much about what we should learn but how we should equip ourselves to learn. Many employees, as well as good souls caught in the manic mire of today's relationships, would gladly learn whatever they must to be able to perform with a sense of ease and security. That knowledge cannot, however, be handed to them or accessed from libraries or the Internet. The knowledge we need is not knowledge that exists outside ourselves. Rather, it is internal knowledge, understanding, and accessibility of our own thinking and learning processes.

For the first time in human history, self-knowledge, in a purely practical sense, is critical to success and survival. The legitimate definition of (and requisite for) continuous learning is self-learning and self-development. We cannot learn new ways of working, take on new and then newer tasks, or manage the sheer volume of work without undoing and redoing old ways of thinking and perceiving. Nor can we think a creative thought or maintain a human relationship.

Under the pressure of old perceptual constructs, we are still "efforting" our way through the average day and suffering as a result. Effort—once rewarded with 10 extra marks—no longer cuts it. However, effort, *plus* self-managed mental acuity and creativity is the recipe of the crème de la crème. Successful modern entrepreneurs do not take more courses or flip through training flyers to ascertain what they should do next, nor do their inspired employees. These creative thinkers access data (left-brain activity) and innovate (right-brain activity) until they have a sound insight, and then they take calculated risks.

Another example: Saturn encourages its employees to regularly tear apart and rebuild a dummy car. They are told to take what they know into the process and then to suspend their assumptions and "play" at making the car better. All ideas are tried and tested, and the combination of accumulated knowledge and enforced fun (an inducement to literal and neurological creativity), in a trusting group context, makes for unprecedented innovation. Moreover, these innovation sessions leave employees relaxed and committed to principles of quality and production, as well as to each other. No one is told what to do or how to do it. Nor are they told that they had better change. There are no threats of penalties (the old best way to create an atmosphere of disincentive). Rather, they are encouraged to think differently, to take risks, and to challenge what they once thought (just last year!) was the best way to put together a great car. The process does more than merely pay lip service to participation. Rather, it leaves participants with a sense of ownership.

To assume that employees will undergo personal and professional transformations by virtue of merely being gathered together to contribute to or endorse a mission or vision statement is cruel and expensive sophistry. Without an intelligently and courageously directed transformation of an organizational culture, including a redefinition of work and of personal, mental, and emotional commitments, there remain employees addressing tasks the old way with a new and speciously promising mandate hanging over their heads. And it is over their heads, unless they are supportively convinced that the onus is on themselves to make personal and professional mental shifts and to self-evaluate in order to do so.

Undoing to Do

Clearly, we have to undo what are, through no fault of our own, currently disastrous applications of another, albeit recent era. We need a specific process of personal mental evaluation, of decoding and encoding perceptual constructs to quell the madness and induce a flexible way of thinking that ensures successful, resourceful endeavors.

One possibility is a process I have taught employee populations across North America, an exercise in organizational and individual refurbishment. It is highly successful at both levels if the powers-that-be sincerely endorse it as the thread running through organizational performance mandates and if they insist that it be continued and reviewed in group settings as part of the commitment requirements (not the job description) of each employee and manager. I have also taught the technique without a buy-in from management, and in these instances, many individuals have benefited enormously by choosing to self-manage in solo.

In other words, regardless of whether our organizations and social-educational institutions are prepared to bite the cultural and cognitive bullet, we can learn the fundamentals of self-management on our own. In fact, it is incumbent upon us to do so.

The process I use, which I call Mental Housecleaning, comprises four simple steps.

1. Listen to and become aware of your encoding, historic thinking, or self-talk. Do this for about a week to 10 days.
2. Establish the origin and accuracy of the thinking. Do this by yourself. It is your voice and opinion that you believe.
3. Interrupt the encoding thinking by saying "cancel!" to yourself with intensity. And replace the negative program with a positive and reasonable affirmation.
4. Repeat the positive and reasonable affirmation until it becomes habitual.

Each of these steps is explained below.

Listen to the Coded Thinking

First, we have to be attentive to and evaluate our thinking. Our emotionality, the activity of which is centered in the amygdala of the brain, can be interrupted by self-directed thinking. Our precoded emotionality can also be coded and recoded by related habitual thinking (as it has been for years). If we merely listen to what we are saying to ourselves—thinking about ourselves, our environments, our predicaments, and so on—we get a clarifying look at and explanation for our anxiety, depression, fear, and anger.

All emotionality is preceded by a thought or thoughts. By simply listening to our thinking, which supports our internal and external perceptual postures, we can get more than a hint of why we feel the way we do in certain situations, why we are good at certain things, why we avoid others, and why we like certain kinds of people more than others.

Since childhood, we have, via our thinking (acquired initially from the thinking of those around us), been coding ourselves—or loading mental software and transferring most of it to our hard drives or subconscious. In that we have done all this unconsciously, we are at the mercy of our early, resilient, and compounded programming until we listen to what we are messaging to ourselves.

We have been sending and receiving the same messages, relevant or irrelevant, realistic or unrealistic, accurate or inaccurate, for a lifetime. And as a result of our deft ability to self-program, we have acquired the neurophysiologic propensity for finding external data to support our belief-based emotionality. We have this propensity for the simple reason that we are programmed to notice only what fits into our precoded perceptual constructs. Anything else is distorted so it *also* fits the program.

For example, if someone believes that people in general are lazy, she will consciously and subconsciously notice and seek out only information that supports that belief. Even if she is with the most diligent hardworking group of people on the planet, what she will notice and file is evidence to the contrary: a random yawn, someone squirming in his chair, someone else's taking two bathroom breaks in an hour, and the natural, responsible (but misinterpreted) performance of other incumbencies. In fact, the everyone-is-lazy mental posture is a perfect example of a driving, organizationally destructive perceptual construct that guarantees perpetual displeasure and frustration on the part of its holder. Moreover, employees have no way to fix the problem of the boss's displeasure. Regardless of what they do, all real or imaginary evidence pertaining to laziness and irresponsibility will be gleaned and groomed by precoded, preprogrammed expectations.

The good news is that if we merely listen to and become aware of our thinking (interrupt the habit), we slow down distorting and self-limiting thinking. A study conducted at the University of Waterloo, Ontario, showed that an individual's overall stress (caused by habitual, inner perceptions and reactions to external stressors) is reduced by approximately 30 percent within a week simply by monitoring otherwise powerfully programmed thinking. Dr. David Burns, of the Cognitive Foundation, University of Pennsylvania Medical School, has ascertained the same and more. He and others have established, without an iota of doubt, that we can transform our inner and outer worlds simply by managing our thinking—that is, by ascertaining what is real, sensible, and useful and what is not in our personal programming.

This awareness of our habitual thinking is the first step in undoing what makes us misdo, what cripples us when it comes to much needed individual change.

Establish Origin and Accuracy

The second step, ideally started after a week to 10 days of self-monitored thinking, is to evaluate specific aspects of our thinking for both origin and accuracy. As already indicated, we acquired our thinking from somewhere, usually from salient people in our early lives, who were doing the best they could at the time. Once we ascertain a consistent theme in our self-talk self-programming—say, the idea that "I am stupid"—we need to know where the belief originated. Did it come from a demanding parent, an early teacher, sibling teasing? We have to discover where the beliefs originated in order to lead the subconscious through a process of deprogramming. Unless we start with how and when the software was installed, we cannot remove it.

Next we have to confront ourselves with whether or not the belief is accurate. That's easier said than done in a culture that condones self-deprecation and spurns mere pride of accomplishment. Yet being clear with and in ourSelves regarding our strengths and weaknesses is basic to our being able to approach our lives and the world with sane thinking.

This step can be fundamentally if positively disruptive. It requires that we look at thinking that is not working, that is causing us to do the same thing over and over again with negative or unsatisfactory results (one clinical definition of insanity). So, when we confront thinking that tells us that we are, for example, stupid, we have to ask ourselves, unabashedly, whether we really are or are not, and what need was or has been supported by the belief. Has it helped us to escape obligations, provided an excuse to avoid higher education, or perhaps just enabled us to feel okay about contributing nothing in meetings? Whatever need was filled can tell us much about the accuracy or inaccuracy of the belief and related, supportive thinking.

Other common examples of beliefs supported by daily programming are "I should never take risks"; "I should be seen not heard"; "I have nothing to offer that others do not already know"; "I am too unattractive to draw attention to myself"; "I am useless at sports ... I am no good with people ... I can't make presentations ... I haven't got a creative bone in my body"; and so on. All can be examples of inaccurate beliefs that need to be recognized as such and then deprogrammed accordingly.

Two caveats are needed here. First, what if we find we have a belief that is true but not deleterious to ourSelves? Perhaps I hear myself thinking "I am no good at sports" but can say, with scrupulous honesty, "So what? It makes no difference in the way I approach life." In such a situation, the best advice is an old engineers' maxim: "If it ain't broke, don't fix it."

Second, what if we have a belief that is accurate but not useful? For example, I had a patient who had lost a leg to cancer. His belief, supported by his self-talk, was that he was a "gimp." As a result, everything he did, he did as a "gimp," and he perceived everyone as relating to him as a "gimp." If he did not get a job, it was because of his disability. So was a woman's declining a dinner date.

The fact of his disability was accurate. However, the realities he had created around it were not necessarily accurate, and they certainly were not useful. He had colored his world with his pervading, self-defining preoccupation with his handicap.

I counseled him to manage his thinking by eliminating his inner chatter and angry self-recrimination regarding his handicap. In other words, the belief was technically accurate, but it was not useful to allow it to define (and make excuses for) his life experiences. His belief, preoccupation, and polluted thinking were the *real* handicap.

In short, this was a perfect example of a self-concept that was real but could, with managed thinking, be made much less consequential and limiting than it would otherwise be.

Interrupt Coded Thinking, and Replace

The third step in the process of mental housecleaning is twofold: interrupting the negative coded thinking; and immediately substituting a more reasonable or accurate thought.

After having become aware of inner dialogues that are sustaining inaccurate or deleterious beliefs, we are able to either sense them coming or know when we are most likely to resort to them. As we continue to be aware of our thinking, we can be vigilant against these thoughts, and as they emerge, jump on them immediately.

We do this by "hearing" the thought come—or even start—and then mentally truncating it with a powerful word such as *cancel*. (Some people find it effective to use a double disburser, such as *"Cancel! Cancel!"*.) Then, virtually within the same breath, we replace the old, debilitating programming with a new and accurate alternative phrase.

For example, if I tell myself periodically that I am stupid, I hear (more accurately, "feel") that thought coming, instantly say "Cancel, cancel," and then, in the same second and a half, say with power and conviction, "I am an intelligent and competent gal!" I might even say it again with a change in word emphasis and tonality and with even more conviction. This simple process, done often enough, not only interrupts what was once ongoing, unconscious self-programming for stupidity. It also reprograms me for intelligence by forming a new belief.

Done with diligence and commitment, the replacement programming does not take very long. We can undo in six months what it took a lifetime to acquire and sustain. For individuals who are highly motivated—those with a terminal illness or recovering from cardiac failure, for example—the process can take significantly less time. Regardless, the neurophysiologic effects are felt within a week or two. Considering that we experience and sustain most of our mind-body stress from the inside out, it is not surprising that as soon as we interrupt our belief system and start to change it, we feel differently. We also begin to behave in a new way and to be perceived somewhat differently by others. (People are likely to ask what we have been doing: a workout, a new diet, an involvement with a new person?)

Although the effects are soon noticeable in our external world, the change is actually taking place in our defining, motivating, and directing inner world. Taking on one, two, or three major but debilitating beliefs at a time and staying on top of them is neurologically and physically cleansing. So it is no wonder that we begin to feel different ourselves and that we begin to appear different to others. We are changing, breaking out of old mindsets and automatically becoming more open, seeing things we never saw before and approaching fundamental aspects of our lives with more flexibility and less resistance.

Repeat

The last but ongoing step is repetition. We must, whenever we think of it, preoccupy ourselves with the new thought pattern. A helpful trick is to tie the new statement to some familiar, frequently repeated action, such as jogging or simply walking from parking lot to coffeeshop or elevator to office. We can fit the affirmation into the rhythm of our movement, just as we had done before, unconsciously, with the old programming. This approach sounds silly (in fact, the entire process seems unnatural) only because we have never before been in the driver's seat of our own thinking. In fact, we are experts at this process. We have been doing it our entire lives without being conscious of it. All we are doing differently is choosing what we will allow in, as inner programming, and discarding what we will not. We are taking control of a process that we once allowed to run out of control.

Top competitive athletes and high achievers with well-rounded, successful lives have invariably learned to manage their inner worlds and external abilities this way. The rest of us, until thinking skills are taught in a saner, more pertinent educational system, have to learn on our own—or, if we are lucky, under the aegis of intelligent workplace leadership.

Estimating Prognosis and Potential

The process of housecleaning increases mental acuity (clarity and precision), as well as flexibility, creativity, and efficiency. If we eliminate inaccurate, misdirecting, and counterproductive beliefs by adjusting our thinking in support of new, helpful or resourceful beliefs, we naturally undergo a process of renewal.

Of course, it is never completed once and for all. Just as we would never stick with 20- or 30-year-old software or hardware to run and direct our computers, we cannot do so with our thinking and perceptual concepts. In fact, given life's ups and downs and resultant mental diversions, we will probably find that we have to cognitively deprogram and reprogram for further growth every few years. If someone hurts us, if we suffer a loss, or if we become ill, we will want to go through the process again, with beginner's diligence. As the expression goes, "Shit happens." And when it does, it shakes our inner worlds. However, it is our "response-ability" to manage the thoughts and feelings related to whatever happens to us and to direct and define the final effect on our psyches and character.

I have taught this housecleaning process often enough to be reasonably savvy about the prospects of everyone's adopting it with immediate fervor and ongoing enthusiasm. As indicated earlier, I am most heartened when individuals *have* to learn it as part of a mandate for growth and change. Most of us find it strange and awkward to consciously play around in our own heads. Individuals whose only incentive is a vague hope of feeling and performing better will probably find it easier to take ginseng. However, those who are sufficiently fed up with the course of their lives, who suffer a sense of confusion, loss of purpose, anger, guilt, or sadness, or who find themselves chronically under the weather, can find answers and relief in the process, earnestly embarked on. Unless something is seriously, medically wrong, we are usually the ones who put ourselves out with our own thinking or directives. If we become sufficiently miserable as a result of the unmanaged mess in our inner worlds, we can face it and change it. But the misery inherent in coping with each day has to be greater than the misery of the awkwardness of challenging our own belief system.

With personal, resourceful self-programming, we get to see who and what we are in terms of talents and abilities. Instead of accepting a view from our personal history, externally and internally fed, we can be authentically ourselves. In fact, the process is so powerfully liberating of our true Selves that most of us end up healthily reviewing much of what we have done with and in our lives. Even our relationships seem different— better or worse. If we have committed ourselves to loving someone with, for example, false beliefs about our own worthiness, reprogramming may lead to deciding that we want to revise the circumstances. In work situations, if we ascertain that our programming has, in the past, made us fear authority, we will probably become much more outspoken and at ease.

Regardless of the particular beliefs and outcomes, we undergo a personal transformation when we replace old programming. Far from being frightening, the process is sanity-inducing. We start to live life as it is, rather than as our negative programming has made us experience it. We become infinitely less judgmental, superstitious, racist, hypercritical, and dumb. And invariably, we find ourselves connecting more often with more people in qualitatively better ways. The critical human issues discussed in relation to the other 12 principles in this book become much less problematic as we become Selves freed from the deprivatory vice of past and present programming.

Once we have control of our own mind and heart, we can choose how we will react and whether or not, for example, we will trust and love. Finding that we have made a mistake becomes much less of a near-death experience in that we are much less prone to be self-punitive. We are also significantly less likely to project old programming onto other people who are innocent or merely fallible. Responsive, not reactive, we can maintain a relatively sanguine inner world, assuredly dressed down for success.

This human, social, and industrial revolution requires that we quietly but concertedly storm our own brains. It is a thinking revolution requiring a leap of cognitive and emotive power. An exciting journey, it requires a commitment to the management of and involvement in the quality of our lives. And the manifold benefits bring the promise of the greatest security of all: self-knowledge. With the unreality of who and what we are out of the way, virtually anything is possible, including the lightening of what has, for many, been a lifelong wrestle between life and living.

CASE STUDY

Mark Learns Self-Management the Hard Way

Mark was the typical whiz kid. He joined an internationally renowned law firm at age 25 and after six years had risen through the ranks to a partnership. By then he had a wife and three children under 10, an elegant apartment in a large urban center, and a palatial weekend retreat a mere 45 minutes away. His children were fit, handsome, and in expensive private schools that guaranteed them an edge on the future. His family regularly traveled without him—to Europe, to Greece, to Aspen—wherever his wife thought would be educational or healthy for the children.

During the early 1990s, law firms all over North America started to scramble for big and bigger accounts. Mark had always brought in more than his share, but he felt that he wasn't as effective under the new market conditions as he had been as he rose in the company. Worried, even frightened, he started to put in even longer hours, sometimes going without sleep, in an attempt to get back to where and who he had been and what he had been able to produce.

Circumstances had changed so drastically, however, that his once tried and true methods of scoring with clients were not nearly as effective as they had been. The firm's senior partner spoke to him about trying other approaches and being a bit more creative in his work. Mark agreed but didn't have the faintest idea what his boss meant. He just kept working harder, becoming more and more frustrated and eventually angry with himself, the firm, clients, his family, and life itself. He worked feverishly every night and every weekend, but he still could not meet his earlier record.

As Mark's temper rose, so did his blood pressure. And one afternoon, after bemoaning the fact that all he did was work, getting nowhere, he collapsed. He had a minor stroke combined with a massive heart attack.

Mark's family background offered no history of heart disease. Moreover, he was a runner (a Type A runner, as in "I have to run"), he worked out, he ate healthily, he had never smoked, and he restricted his drinking to the odd glass of wine at a company dinner. In the hospital, after the terror had worn off, becoming just high-grade daily fear, Mark felt persecuted. He was angry that he, of all people, had been struck down this way. But it was evident to all in the postcardiac care clinic that Mark had a poor prognosis if he did not change his ways—especially his posture toward work and life—from the inside out.

Throughout his life, Mark had worked from a place of inner anger. His wife had always seen it. His children had born the brunt of it. And he himself had once succeeded because and in spite of it. Whatever he did, he did in order to be better, to not fail, and to stay one step ahead of a cataclysm. His automatic thinking (self-talk) had encoded him since childhood for a self-punitive competitiveness that kept him tight, tense, and intense. In fact, his mental recovery process eventually revealed that Mark had always approached work and life from a point of defense. He succeeded so as not to fail and won so as to avoid being labeled a loser.

Mark's doctors eventually convinced him that he had to change his mental diet. His anger, an emotion proven directly contributive to heart attacks in men, would kill him if he did not.

While still in the hospital and then as an outpatient, Mark set about getting off his own back. Well motivated (with three young children and a rediscovered love of things other than legal briefs), he went through an intensive mental and emotional housecleaning process whereby he found and eliminated the punitive and assaultive aspects of his constant inner chatter. In a few months, he mastered the process of reprogramming himself for more inner latitude, for self-care, even for self-congratulations. As a result, he learned to perform at work with infinitely less strain and frustration. Moreover, he ceased to model self-punitive success for his children and was much more accessible to his wife.

Today he is just as successful as he ever was (if not more so from a managerial position in his firm). He is also healthier than ever and gives seminars to other angry overworkers, male and female, in an effort to spare them the terror of his brush with death as well as an unnecessarily punitive and painful path to success.

EXERCISE

Use the mental housecleaning process outlined in the main text to examine and start to deprogram thinking that you realize is getting in the way of your success and rapports. Redo the process with each deleterious belief and the related emotions. Then use repetition to remain on top of the old beliefs that are most pervasively detrimental. Note how you feel in two weeks and then after one month. Teach the method to your colleagues if they ask about it or otherwise show interest. Make it part of the way your family grows together.

Conclusion

The 20th-century Argentinean writer Jorge Luis Borges portrays the universe as "a garden of forking paths," with one straight route through time but infinite paths—divergent, convergent, parallel, and cyclical. Each human being's mazelike routes through time and space double back again and again, often as coincidences. We are greeted at every turn by our own reflections, alternate realities, pasts, and futures. Choice—and the courage required to make uneasy choices—are what propel us toward and onto a certain path, to other paths, and then others, with telling reflections of the quality of our journey. Too often, for many of us, the reflections mirror absence and the defeat of selfhood.

We have no substitute for the subjectively managed inclusion of our hearts in our daily endeavors. However, as implied throughout this book, it is ourselves, our hearts that we remove or numb when we are either frenetically rushed or insecure. And in our so-called private lives or in our work lives, the exclusion of heart is a guarantee of failure by default or a mordant inability to contribute. The latter, we all know, can now mean exclusion from the marketplace and the means of production. What counts most is the unique and personal application of our real Selves to real processes and commitments. To play it safe, restricting what we bring to others and to our lives and paying only self-centered, surface attention to a fashionably commodified Selfhood, is to buy into the condoned facility of fraudulence. Yet safe and fake is where many of us have decided to live, as if they were overlapping places where we never have to feel or take responsibility for the quality of our life and the lives of others; where we experience no confusion or a sense of inadequacy; where we always get our share; and where no one can hurt us again. We huddle too long on paths shadowed by a past and times and incidents long gone, in mental spaces that are dim and dank but dustily familiar, like tombs. Indeed, we wait not in happiness but in a barely tolerable, poorly camouflaged state of inner petrification.

As we rush through our necessarily ad-libbed days (and sometimes nights), we barely have time to stop to feel, look, and learn. But if we pause to listen to some of the greatest scientific minds in the world, we can glean guidance. Most are writing and speaking publicly about the necessity of approaching the future from a place in our Selves apparently deleted from our formative pasts. For the chief executive officer of a Fortune 1000 corporation that encourages cutting-edged approaches to innovation, the middle manager caught in petty office feuds, the couple who don't know what happened to the magic in their marriage, or a baby boomer facing a rebellious teenager, the facile application of old belief systems is an act of lazy dishonesty, inadvertent cruelty, and masochism. Our shared challenge is daring to embark on a new path based on an honest reflection of our confusion and insanity. Subconsciously, most of us have just assumed that we can still win—or not lose—by merely applying half our brains, giving nothing of our hearts, and keeping more than half an eye on our backs. But most of us also know (and hide), the fact that we are losing inner ground. Success and sanity come from cognitive sincerity, from heartful, mindful approaches to human and human-created dilemmas.

Scientists, even more than so-called humanists at this point in millennial history, are urging us to dare to become more involved in our own lives and in the lives of others, perhaps because they know what is now our shared potential for self-destruction. Humanists and social scientists understand the implications and consequences of both broken hearts and heartless human endeavors. Without heart and courage, we live non-lives, especially now. We are nervously mesmerized by our manic, mechanical, ratlike use of technology, manipulating ourselves and circumstances to such a speed that we dare not blink for fear of missing a piece of what was once inconsequential data. We all see and know that we have made leisure virtually impossible and love a mere afterthought. We are straining to keep up with lives driven by hardware and software, originally created to give us more time and to ease the burden of devoting the larger part of our lives to earning the "right" to live in comfort. Scientists work with creative diligence to bring an idea to fruition—that is the nature of their work. We have, for the most part, taken the fruits of their labor and blindly applied them to accelerate our lives, not to make them either better or more practical. The erosive effects show and hurt. If we are going to work and live at what anthropologists and psychologists submit is a humanely impossible pace, then we had better take stock and care—in areas and reflections simpler and more directly related to life.

We all pick up enough split-second reportage from our car radios to be aware of the fact that we are becoming meaner people. Even amid the ubiquitous noise, unconsciously contrived to keep us from having to endure the telling susurrations of silence, we hear sound bites related to our shared behavior. We hear that road rage is now an official psychological condition affecting more than 85 percent of us who drive, and we hear that our children are looking to other children for bonding and affirmation, often manifested in intimately loyal acts of violence. When we hear that some of them have, again this month, shot each other in the onetime sanctity of a schoolyard, we cringe between a multitude of incompletable tasks.

We hear these things, albeit peripherally, and lower our heads into our already unnaturally heightened shoulders, human turtles trying to recede from what we know is too painful to fully receive. We know—and have known for a while—that we, in our quiet, busy ways, have been making the news. Highway, schoolyard, and rec room shootings are too comprehensible for words already left unspoken, as is the naturally explosive anger born of loneliness and separation.

Fundamental Principles

If the principles set out in this book seem simple, self-evident, and even fundamentally archaic, then the reader has read them as I meant them to be. I promised at the beginning of this book that it would not be another "steps for success" book with specious strategies for instant happiness and better living. Discussions of this sort are now the grossly popular tasks of others. The principles I offer are meant to be seriously pondered and applied just as they are, as barebone, hard and fast principles related to human decency, choice, survival, and growth.

We are, most of us, kind creatures when we are not afraid. And most of us are as hungry for love as we are to be loved. The principles are reminders of the real reasons for our emptiness, our allegiance to a growing cult of meanness, and our torn if cosmetically attractive lives. They are also irrefutably passages to our return to sane living, to healthier, more beautiful paths, and to the richness of responsible contribution.

In the era in which we find ourselves, we can accomplish and create to a degree greater than in any period in human history. However, we can also fake frantic participation, smother our souls, and lose our Selves. We must beware of the danger inherent in the popularization and passive acceptance of simulated sanguinity and memorized wisdom. All of us have to, as a right and a necessity, apply our Selves from our separate places of uniqueness and heart. As participants giving from beyond the acceptable level of buzz phrases and bland but safe uniformity, we can both enrich our own worthy lives and bring real human value to our organizations. Ironically, in the most transitional, high-tech period in human evolution, we serve each other well by reviewing and applying the mere basics of our humanity.

That is where we should be looking for self-managed kindness, creativity, and healthy resilience. Globally, organizationally, and individually, we need to cease looking elsewhere and look to our Selves for the ways and means of modern living. We need to be less impressed with the barbaric fact that we can clone ourselves than with the equally barbaric fact that we are blithely breaking, rather than nurturing, each other's hearts.

Epilogue

It is not seeing with the eye but seeing with the mind that gives us a basis for belief, and in this way science and religion are one. We are now entering an age when we will hold the power of life in our hands, and if it is to be used properly, it must be in a world dominated by love. What we must have in the world today is a chain reaction of the human spirit. If we can feel this vision and if we can act on it, if we can transmit this vision to others and persuade everyone that living in terms of the spirit, and of love is the only answer, then we can change the face of the world.

Dr. Donald Hatch Andrews,
professor of chemistry, Johns Hopkins University

Suggested Reading

Anderson, Greg. *Life on Purpose*. San Francisco: Harper, 1997.

Argyris, Chris. "Empowerment: The Emperor's New Clothes." *Harvard Business Review*, May/June 1998.

Bartlett, C.A., and S. Ghoshal. "Changing the Role of Top Management: Beyond Strategy to Purpose," *Harvard Business Review*, 72 (2, 1996).

Bennis, Warren. *On Becoming a Leader*. Reading, Mass.: Addison-Wesley, 1997.

————. *Managing People Is Like Herding Cats*. S. Provo, Calif.: Cynthia Langley Publishing, 1997.

Bennis, Warren, and Burt Manus. *Leaders—The Strategies for Taking Charge*. Toronto: Harper and Row, 1986.

Chopra, D. *Quantum Healing*. New York: Bantam Books, 1990.

————. *Ageless Body, Ageless Mind*. New York: Bantam Books, 1993.

————. *The Seven Spiritual Laws of Success*. New York: Amber-Allen Publishing, 1994.

Church, E. "Soul surfaces in the office canyons." *The Globe and Mail*, May 22, 1998.

Coleman, D. *Emotional Intelligence: Why It Can Matter More than I.Q.* New York: Bantam Books, 1995.

Collins, J.C. "Building Your Company's Vision." *Harvard Business Review*, 74 (2, 1996).

Collins, James, and Jerry Porras. *Built to Last*. New York: HarperBusiness, 1994.

Conduct Problems Research Group. "A Developmental and Clinical Model for The Prevention of Conduct Disorder: The Fast Track Program." *Development and Psychopathology*, 4 (1992).

Covey, Steven. *Principle-Centered Leadership*. New York: Simon and Schuster, 1987.

————. *The 7 Habits of Highly Successful People*. New York: Simon and Schuster, 1988.

Csikszentmihalyi, M. *Flow: The Psychology of Optimal Experience*. New York: Harper and Row, 1990.

Davies, P. *The Mind of God, The Scientific Basis for a Natural World*. New York: Simon and Schuster, 1992.

Davis, K. *Getting into the Customer's Head*. New York: Harper Row, 1996.

Dunlap, A.J. *Mean Business*. New York: Times Business, 1996.

Dyer, W. *Manifest Your Destiny*. New York: HarperCollins, 1997.

Elias, M.J., et al. "The Promotion of Social Competence." *American Journal of Orthopsychiatry*, 61 (1991).

Elias, M.J., and J. Chabby. *Building Social Problem-Solving Skills*. San Francisco: Jossey-Bass, 1992.

Epstein, M. *Thoughts without a Thinker*. New York: Basic Books, 1995.

Foundation for Inner Peace. *A Course in Miracles*. New York: Columbia University Press, 1987.

Fromm, E. *When We Were as Gods*. New York: Fawcett, 1950.

Galbraith, John Kenneth. *The Good Society*. New York: Houghton Mifflin, 1996.

Gardner, Howard. *Multiple Intelligences: The Theory in Practice*. New York: Basic Books, 1993.

Grote, Dick. *Discipline without Punishment*. New York: Amacom Books, 1994.

Hall, Doug, and David Wecker. *Jump Start Your Brain*. New York: Warner Books, 1995.

Hillman, James. *The Soul's Code: In Search of Character and Calling*. New York: Random House, 1996.

Jones, L.B. *Jesus—CEO: Using Ancient Wisdom for Visionary Leadership*. New York: Hyperion, 1994.

Kiechet, W. "A Manager's Career in the New Economy." *Fortune*, November 1997.

Kinnon, D. *Leading Change*. Boston: *Harvard Business School Press*, 1996.

Kushner, Harold S. *How Good Do We Have to Be?* New York: Little, Brown, 1997.

Low, Albert. *Zen and Creative Management*. Rutland, Vt.: Charles E. Tuttle, 1992.

McGinnis, G. *Learned Optimism*. New York: Random House, 1991.

Maslach, C., and M.P. Leiter, *The Truth about Burnout*. San Francisco: Jossey-Bass, 1997.

Mills, D.Q., and B. Frieson. *Broken Promises*. Cambridge: Harvard Business School Press, 1996.

Murphy J. *Peace within Yourself*. Las Palos, Calif.: deVorss and Co., 1956.

Najchrzak, A., and Q. Wang. "Breaking the Functional Mindset in Functional Organizations." *Harvard Business Review*, September/October 1996.

O'Toole, J. *Leading Change*. San Francisco: James Bass, 1996.

Pearsall, P. *Making Miracles*. New York: Avon Books, 1991.

Pearsall, P. *Superimmunity*. New York: Avon Books, 1992.

Peck, M. Scott. *The Road Less Traveled and Beyond*. New York: Simon and Schuster, 1997.

Peters, Tom. *Thriving on Chaos*. New York: HarperCollins, 1987.

———. *The Pursuit of WOW!* New York: Vintage Books, 1994.

Peterson, C., and M. Bossio. *Health and Optimism*. New York: MacMillan International, 1991.

Pollard, W.C. *The Soul of the Firm*. New York: HarperBusiness, 1996.

Price-Waterhouse. *Change Integration Team, Better Change*. New York: Irwin Professional Publishing, 1995.

Robbins, Harvey. *Why Teams Don't Work*. Princeton N.J.: Peterson's/Pacesetter Books, 1995.

Robinson, A.G., and S. Stern. *Corporate Creativity*. New York: Berrett-Koehler, 1997.

Ross, I., and G. MacDonald. "Scars from stress cut deep in workplace." *The Globe and Mail*, October 9, 1997.

Searing, Jill A., and Anne B. Lovett. *The Career Prescription*. New York: Prentice Hall, 1995.

Sharp-Paine, Lyn. "Managing for Organizational Integrity." *Harvard Business Review* 72, (2, 1994).

Shore, Allan. *Affect Regulation and the Origin of Self*. St. Claire, NJ: Lawrence-Erlbaum, 1994.

Slavin, M., and D. Friegman. *The Adaptive Design of the Human Psyche*. New York: Guilford Press, 1992.

Soloman, D., et al. "Creating a Caring Community" In A. Dick and J. Patry, *Effective and Responsible Teaching*. San Francisco: Avelon Press, 1992.

Soros, G. "The Capitalist Threat." *Atlantic Monthly*, February 1997.

Sternberg, R.J. *Beyond I.Q.—a Triarchic Theory of Human Intelligence*. Cambridge: Cambridge University Press, 1996.

Tannenbaum, R., and W.H. Schmidt. "How to Choose a Leadership Pattern." *Harvard Business Review*, Business Classics edition, November 1994.

Thomas, D.A., and R.J. Ely. "Making Differences Matter: A New Paradigm." *Harvard Business Review*, September/October 1996.

Tobin, D.R., *The Knowledge-Enabled Organization*. New York: Amacom Books, 1996.

———. *Transformational Learning*. New York: John Wiley and Sons, 1996.

Toffler, Eric. *Power Shift*. New York: Bantam Books, 1990.

Treacy, Michael, and Fred Wiersema. *The Discipline of Market Leaders*. Reading, Mass.: Addison-Wesley, 1995.

Walsh, Neale Donald. *Conversations with God*. New York: G.P. Putman's Sons, 1997.

Waterman, R.H., and B.A. Colland. "Toward a Career-Resilient Workforce." *Harvard Business Review*, 72 (4, 1994).

Williamson, Marianne. *Handbook for the Soul*. New York: Little, Brown, 1997.

Woodhouse, L.J. *Essential Adjustments*. Toronto: University Resources Press, 1994.

Zoglin, R. "The News Wars." *Time Magazine*, October 21, 1996.

Index

managing, 17
projected, 16-17
and self-forgiveness, 13-15, 19
and self-victimization, 18, 19

H

Harvard Business Review, 156
Harvard University, 156
Heart disease, 129, 130, 187, 191, 192
Here & now. *See* Present, orientation to
Holy Spirit, 9, 155
Humiliation, 16, 21, 25, 54, 72, 146, 148, 153-54
Hussein, Saddam, 40

I

Idealization, 19, 85, 105, 107, 108, 109, 111, 150
Imagination, 97, 98, 124
Informer-controller diad, 33-35
Inner awareness, 6-7, 17, 119-20 (*See also* Self-knowledge)
Inner dialogue. *See* Self-dialogue
Inner peace:
case study, 129-30
choice of, xv, 25, 29, 116-31
exercise, 130
(*See also* Stillness)
Insanity, xi, 185
Intimacy, xviii, 55, 56, 74, 84-85, 106, 153
Isolation, xiii, xv, 11, 13, 39-40, 46-49, 51, 53, 56, 57, 59-60, 74, 83, 107, 167

J

Jampolsky, Gerald, 40-41
Judgmental reactivity, 13, 14-15, 23, 41, 51, 52, 54, 58, 59, 60, 61, 62, 72, 73, 101, 141
Jung, Carl, 9, 155
Juvenile crime, 36, 195

K

Kindness, 44, 59, 61, 62, 74, 77-78, 98, 99, 100, 144, 162, 165, 166, 167
K-Mart, 171

L

Leaders, leadership, 52, 56, 59,

63, 64, 89-90,113, 122, 125, 127, 152-53, 168-69, 170-71, 172, 188
Learning organization, 176-77
Lessons (living), 80-90
Letting go:
of mother, 107
of negative feelings, 25
of romantic relationships, 24, 105
(*See also* Detachment)
Life planners, profile of, 138, 142
Life planning, 132-44
case study, 143-44
exercise, 144
Life spirit/force, 138, 155, 156
Lifestyle diseases, 43, 123, 129, 191
Listening:
case study, 158-59
exercise, 160
to inner self, 5, 6-7, 8-9, 17, 56, 64, 75, 94, 97, 98, 100, 123, 145, 155, 157, 183, 184 (*See also* Stillness)
and leadership, 152-53
to nature, 156, 157, 158, 160
to others, 145, 146, 147-55, 157
Living, modern:
challenges of, xi-xiv, 4, 22, 26, 42, 43, 46, 51, 52, 53, 91, 99, 100, 114, 123, 134-35, 180, 194-95
and conflict, 29, 58
and emotionality, 73
and fear, 36, 39-40, 58
and love, 107, 111
and work, xiv, xvi, 51-52, 54, 95-97, 99-100, 112-13, 133-36, 138, 157, 179
Living, momentary. *See* Present, orientation to
Living, successful, principles:
connection vs. dismissal, 65-79
detachment/rationality, 104-15
focus, 91-103
forgiveness/acceptance, 12-31
giving & receiving, 161-72
life planning, 132-44
living lessons, 80-90
observation/judgment, 50-64

peace, choice of, 116-31
real communication, 145-60
self-acceptance, 1-11
self-management, 173-92
Loss, 24-25, 37-39, 41, 107, 114
Love:
early stage, 104, 105-6, 107
false, 104-7
mature, 15, 106, 111, 115
media depiction of, 85, 105, 107, 109
need for, xv, 107, 108, 109-10
proclamations of, 150
search for, 104-5, 108-10
western perception of, 104-6, 108
will to, 50-51, 111
(*See also* Open love; Romantic love; Self-love)
Love Is Letting Go of Fear (Jampolsky), 40-41

M

MacEnroe, John, 121
Marcuse, Herbert, 134
Marriage, 105, 159, 178
Marx, Karl, xvi
Maslow, Abraham, xvi
Materialism, xii, xvi, xviii, 8, 26, 119, 137, 162, 163-64
Maya, 74, 75
Media depictions:
justice, 12
love, 85, 105, 107, 109
success, 134
therapies, 92
violence, 116, 117
Meditation, 9, 17, 28, 98, 124 (*See also* Stillness)
Mental acuity, 180, 181, 188
Mental housekeeping:
benefits of, 188-90, 192
case study, 190-92
exercise, 192
steps, 182-88
Mind/body connection, 54, 60, 121-22, 123, 126-27, 187
Mirroring, 3, 4-5, 23, 50, 51, 53, 54, 58, 61-63, 193
Misbehavior. *See* Behavior, negative
Mission statements, 78, 99-100, 152, 182
(*See also* Personal mission statement; Personal technical plan)
Morality, 125-26, 142